EDVARD MUNCH

ALF BØE

EDVARD MUNCH

RIZZOLI
NEW YORK

PHOTOGRAPHY CREDITS

Museum Behnhaus, Lübeck (fig. 96)

Bergen Billedgalleri & Rasmus Meyers Samlinger, Bergen
(Henriksen A/S) (figs. 17, 22, 111)

Göteborgs Konstmuseum, Gothenburg (fig. 124)

Kunsthaus Zürich (fig. 88)

Moderna Museet, Stockholm (fig. 31)

Nasjonalgalleriet, Oslo (Jacques Lation)
(figs. 12, 15, 16, 18, 24, 39, 54, 58, 148)

Thielska Galleriet, Stockholm (fig. 99)

Fotograf Væring, Oslo
(figs. 38, 131, 128, 129, 130)

All other photographs:
Munch-museet, Oslo (Svein Andersen)

First published in the United States of America in 1989 by

RIZZOLI INTERNATIONAL PUBLICATIONS, INC.

300 Park Avenue South, New York, NY 10010

© 1989 Ediciones Polígrafa, S. A.
Translated from the Norwegian by Robert Ferguson

Library of Congress Cataloging-in-Publication Data

Bøe, Alf.
    [Edvard Munch.   English]
    Edvard Munch
        p.   cm.
    Translation of: Edvard Munch.
    Bibliography: p.
    Includes index.
    ISBN 0-8478-1077-1
    1. Munch, Edvard, 1863-1944.   2. Artists—Norway—Biography.
I. Munch, Edvard, 1863-1944.   II. Title.
N7073.M8B6413 1989
760'.092'4—dc 19   89-3780
                                                          CIP

Printed and bound in Spain by La Polígrafa, S. A.
Parets del Vallès (Barcelona)
Dep. Leg. B. 15.329 - 1989

CONTENTS

Photo of Munch on his 80th birthday, 12 December 1943. Munch Museum.

Introduction

Fourteen days after the German army invaded Norway, on April 9 1940, Edvard Munch wrote his last will and testament. He was then a frail old man, almost 77 years old, and under those grave and fateful circumstances passed on his instructions in broad statements. His entire oeuvre, which surrounded him in his home, was bequeathed to the city of Oslo. More than 1,100 canvases, thousands of drawings and sketchbooks, all of his graphic works (numbering more than 800 different motifs represented by a series of proof impressions and duplicates from different editions), his photographs, manuscripts, and private notes — everything was left to the city in which he had spent his childhood and adolescence. There, too, he had settled, an established artist known world-wide, during the first world war to live out the remainder of his life. He knew quite well what he was doing; as he told his friend Christian Gierløff during a conversation at Ekely in the last years of his life, "It will only become really interesting when all of the work can be considered and compared in a single context — all of the studies and all of the sketches, together with the finished works, through all the different stages."

His letters were left to his sister Inger, and upon her death these were added to the collection. The city built a museum to house it, so that all of the material has been accessible to an international public since it opened in 1963. The breadth and depth and sheer size of this collection provide an opportunity to study an individual modern artist's life and work that is, in all probability, unique.

Scholars who have been responsible for the surge of interest in Edvard Munch in recent years have been able to use the collection as their chief source. The life and work of the artist have been examined in a number of extensive general works; specialized studies have concentrated on individual aspects or problematic areas, and research has grown to international proportions.

My own involvement with Munch became personal when I took over as director of the museum in Oslo some twelve years ago. I had previously lived in an apartment which looked out across his estate at Ekely on the edge of the city, and had come across people who had known Munch personally and had anecdotes to tell — but it was my encounter with his entire life's work which made an overwhelming impression on me.

The administrative pressures of the museum director's post make it hardly possible for one to become involved with the available material to the extent that a scholar can; on the other hand, the position affords one the pleasures of facilitating such an involvement for others, and of participating in the organization of the many international exhibitions based on loans from the Munch Museum. Furthermore, as custodian of the Munch collection, one has in any case a daily contact with documents, letters and works of art which give one a more intimate knowledge of Munch the man than would have been possible for any of his contemporaries. Munch himself realized that such a situation was inevitable, although his own attitude towards the scholarly investigation of his personal life by future generations was clearly ambivalent. On the cover of one of his journals he wrote: "To be burned"; but as early as September 1932 this was crossed out and replaced by: "To be read by understanding and broad-minded men after my death." Together with my colleagues, I hope that I may be counted among these understanding and broad-minded men. The observations which I can offer are based on my day-to-day familiarity with the artist's collected works and are influenced by colleagues both at home and abroad who have been able to devote time to a more fundamental study of the material than I have been able to undertake.

Edvard Munch: the man

I would like to begin my essay with a description of the man Edvard Munch. We are familiar with him from his own pictorial world, since he was one of those artists who hold up a mirror to their own face throughout their lives, and he has left us with a series of unusual self-portraits. Besides, his was to a high degree an egocentric art, and in countless different contexts he has introduced in his motifs a representation of himself. The Munch collection contains a series of photographs taken with a self-release shutter, as well as numerous pictures of the artist taken by others, showing him in all the different stages of his life, from the pale, sensitive five-year-old in the family portrait of 1868 (Ill. p. 9) to the emaciated old man in his wicker chair a short while before his death in 1944 (Ill. p. 6).

Munch has been described as an extremely handsome man, fair, blue-eyed, straight-backed, a man with a rather aristocratic air. The reality, however, was a little more complicated. He was, indeed, on his father's side, descended from a line of artists, intellectuals, clergymen, and public servants which was reckoned among the most prominent in the land in nineteenth-century Norway, and he was very conscious of this pedigree. It made an "insider" of him, he "belonged." Yet at the same time he was an "outsider." His father Christian Munch was a poor regimental doctor who did not to any considerable extent move in the social circles to which the family naturally belonged. Moreover, he had to some degree cut himself off further by his marriage to the young daughter of a ship's captain — a misalliance, by contemporary standards.

Munch himself evidently saw his parents' marriage thus. Among his papers is a manuscript which describes just such a marriage, in clear reference to their situation. Nevertheless, he felt that much of his strength derived from his mother's side of the family. His maternal grandfather, Andreas Bjølstad, was an impressive and powerful person, and to Ludvig Ravensberg, a young relative, Edvard is said to have remarked that "by day I am Munch, and by night, Bjølstad."

Munch had other reasons to feel that his was in some ways a split personality: the family were orthodox Protestants, and — particularly after the death of Munch's mother in 1868 — there were times when Christian Munch's religious fervor expressed itself in a dark brooding of almost pathological intensity. Edvard himself abandoned the security of his childhood faith at an early age as a result of his contacts with a group of radical intellectuals, something which caused him to struggle, probably for most of the rest of his adult life, with the problem of finding a new philosophical basis for his attitude towards life's mysteries. Munch's contacts with these young radicals, and the freethinking intellectual attitudes he developed, were a source of great distress to his father and led to a worsening of the relationship between the two, which caused Munch regret in later life.

Nevertheless, as Ingrid Langaard has pointed out, the frequent description of Munch's home as "oppressive and joyless" is by no means accurate. She cites the young relative Ludvig Ravensberg's happy memories of his visits to what he called "this noble, poor home, with its dignified atmosphere, its spirituality and its culture," and points to Ravensberg's description of the old army doctor's friendliness, sense of humor, and liveliness, qualities which balanced his somber side.

It was a home with a great deal to offer. Even though Munch's first Norwegian biographer, his friend Jens Thiis, writes that Munch was not a keen reader as a boy, we know that the values of literature were impressed upon him at home; that he had a lively interest in the work of Henrik Ibsen and other contemporary Norwegian writers; and that he devoured Dostoevsky's novels as soon as they appeared in Norwegian and Danish translations from the 1880s onwards. Among his friends, Munch was considered well-read; we know also that he was versed in classical mythology and to some extent in the literature of antiquity. Norwegian history and the Sagas were familiar to him, not least through the work of his own uncle: although the two men never met, Munch was well aware of the importance of P. A. Munch, probably the most notable historian Norway has yet produced. Both his own reading and his various literary friendships were of great importance in providing a thematic basis for Edvard Munch's art.

His milieu and family background provided Munch with a decidedly tense and nervous disposition, with elements of melancholy. His Finnish colleague, the painter Axel Gallén-Kallela, is one among several who point to "the dreadful angst . . . which plagues him" during the 1890s. And the aging Munch himself described for Professor Schreiner that "fear of life which has persecuted me since the day I was born. My art has been like the distress calls broadcast by a radio operator from a sinking ship." Throughout his adult life Munch complained about his nerves, and, increasingly, about the difficulties ordinary human intercourse posed for him. For a time alcohol functioned as his bridge to social life, but with insignificant exceptions he stopped drinking altogether after his nervous breakdown in 1908-9.

During the 1890s Munch's art was considered highly unusual by critics at home. In the words of the Munch Museum's chief curator, Arne Eggum, he was "classified as one of those artists who notoriously overstep the boundary between sanity and madness. It was said that his paintings displayed a pathological over-sensitivity, and his art was characterized as neurotic." His own observation, found among his papers after his death, is well known: "I inherited two of mankind's most deadly enemies — the heritage of consumption and insanity. Sickness, Madness and Death were the black angels who stood round my cradle at birth." Strong words indeed, yet they must be balanced by the testimony of other witnesses. That Munch's behavior — particularly during his drinking bouts — was at times such as to raise doubts about his sanity is probable. He suffered also from agoraphobia and, as we have seen, found ordinary social intercourse difficult. But he was certainly not mad, and there is evidence from those who knew him well of a lighter side to his personality. He had the gift of ironic self-deprecation and a sharp tongue that made him a master of repartee, and he could be high-spirited and very funny. His friend Gustav Schiefler gives us this picture of a life-loving Munch in his journal entry for January 1 1906: "I was heartily pleased by Munch's company. His slim body, with the sharply drawn profile, dressed in sports clothes, a little to the side of me, walked through the forest singing Norwegian songs." Another contemporary observer was Arthur Kahane, Max Reinhardt's dramaturge. He got to know Munch in 1906 when they worked together on a production of Ibsen's *Ghosts* at Max Reinhardt's theater in Berlin. He described him as a fair Nordic Viking, a lonely man who remained very much of a mystery. But there was also about him "something of the child and of the native, an animalistic primitivity, almost;

Photo of Edvard Munch's mother with children (from left to right) Sophie, Andreas, Inger, Edvard and Laura. 1868. Munch Museum.

The wicker chair depicted by Munch in *The Sick Child* and *Death in the Sickroom*, figs. 11 and 57. Munch Museum.

a Parsifalian innocence. And, then again, this incredible complexity, this knowledge of deep secrets.'' Add to this that Munch was well-read, with a highly developed critical faculty, and we have a picture of a complex personality, and an artist who in his work ranged from *The Sick Child* (fig. 11) to caricatures of his previous sweetheart (fig. 102); from the depiction of the introverted and sorrowing figures in *Melancholy (Jappe on the Beach)* from the early 1890s

(fig. 28) to the celebration of masculine power in *Men Bathing* from 1907 (fig. 115).

Although the fundamentals of a personality do not alter, it is obvious that Munch, like everyone else, changed and developed throughout his life, and that these processes were reflected in his art. Before we look into this more closely, however, let us first give a short account of the artist's career, focusing on the pivotal points of his life.

Life and career in brief

On November 8 1880, Edvard Munch wrote in his journal: ''I have once again left the Technical College. It is now my firm intention to become a painter.'' He immediately enrolled in evening classes at the Drawing School in Kristiania, which the capital of Norway was then called. (Its name was changed to Oslo in 1924.) He made rapid progress and was regarded as one of the school's most promising pupils. The school's drawing and life classes were later supplemented by tuition with an older artist friend, Christian Krohg, and periods at a summer school under Frits Thaulow. This, along with a short session at Joseph-Léon Bonnat's art school in Paris in the autumn of 1889, was the full extent of Munch's formal training.

We know at least some of the influences to which he was exposed during his first nine years as a provincial artist, between the ages of 17 and 26. The first Chair in Fine Arts had been established in Norway in 1875, and young Edvard attended the lectures. He studied reproductions of the great paintings of the world, enjoyed access to magazines devoted

to art, and became familiar with the modest collection of works on display at the capital's National Gallery. He attended exhibitions and kept abreast of the latest news and developments from Paris through friends who had been there. In the summer of 1885 he paid a brief visit to the city himself, taking in the World Exhibition at Antwerp en route. Thus he was able to acquire through his gallery visits a general impression of the state of contemporary art, and to study the works of the great masters at first hand. As we shall see, these influences were immediately reflected in his own paintings. He probably visited the great exhibition of Impressionist art at Durand-Ruel in Paris, in which Monet, Morisot, Pissarro, Renoir, Degas, Seurat, Signac, and Sisley were all represented. Many of these he would have seen again at the large exhibition in Copenhagen, which he visited in the summer of 1888, as well as works by Puvis de Chavannes, Raffaëlli, Bastien Lepage, and Delacroix.

Artistic life in Kristiania was provincial, but dominated by the activities of a group of rebellious young open-air

The beach at Åsgårdstrand, where Munch painted the chief motifs of his *Life Frieze* and bought a house in 1897.
Period photo. Munch Museum.

Munch's house in Åsgårdstrand, which he bought in 1897. The house still stands as a museum.
Munch Museum.

painters and by no means lacking in intellectual and artistic vigor. This state of affairs is clearly reflected in Munch's earliest work. Just as important was the influence of a group of socially radical anarchists under the leadership of the writer Hans Jæger. Jæger was a Hegelian, an advocate of free love, and a fierce opponent of the prevailing social structure based on the idea of the family. His very personal literary style influenced Munch, as did his uncompromising insistence that the artist should use the experiences and understandings of his own life as the basis for his art. His credo — "One should write one's life" — was adopted by Munch and applied to painting. A notorious egocentric, Munch put his own life experiences into his art, revealing in the process his life's most private aspects in the hope that his work might function as an aid and an inspiration to others.

The year 1889 marked a turning-point in Munch's life. In October that year he travelled to Paris on a scholarship from the Norwegian government. Thus began a phase of his life which was to last until 1909. It was characterized by constant travel between Norway and other countries, chiefly France and Germany, with shorter and longer stays in Norway most years until 1905. The picturesque little fishing village of Åsgårdstrand on the Oslo fjord became his home base, and in 1897 he bought a small fisherman's cottage by the stony beach which was to prove a source of lasting joy (Ill. p. 10). The long, curving shoreline appears regularly in his paintings from 1889 onwards (Ill. p. 10). His affection for the landscape was such that in later life he felt, when wandering there, as if he were stepping into one of his own canvases.

The importance of this first, three-year stay in France in Munch's artistic development will be discussed later; here it is enough to point out that by the time of his first appearance on the international scene, at the exhibition in Berlin in the autumn of 1892, Munch was already painting in a new, decorative style under the influence of French art. Between 1895 and 1898 he again visited France, where he did his first woodcuts and exhibited at the Bing Gallery. After 1900 he also showed his work at l'Indépendent, of which he became a member in 1903.

While traveling back and forth between France and Germany in the 1890s he extended his circle of friends and acquaintances, among whom probably the most important were those artists and intellectuals who gathered round the Swedish writer August Strindberg (fig. 31) in Berlin. Here he established friendships with, among others, Julius Meier-Graefe, later to become a leading art-historian and author. Meier-Graefe wrote the first serious critical study of Munch. This was published in 1894 in the book *Das Werk des Edvard Munch*, along with articles on Munch by Stanislaw Przybyszewski (fig. 63), Franz Servaes, and Willy Pastor. He was a member of the group involved in the magazine *Pan*, in which some of Munch's work appeared. Munch probably met the architect Henri van de Velde in Berlin and seems to have known him well in his Weimar period after the turn of the century. At that time he also collaborated with Max Reinhardt, and received important support and encouragement from people such as the eye specialist Max Linde from Lübeck, the county court judge Gustav Schiefler in Hamburg, the mystic Albert Kollmann (fig. 88), and the Swedish banker Ernest Thiel, to name but a few.

Throughout this period Munch's life was unstable and uncertain, a life lived under ever-changing circumstances and frequent economic difficulties. There was, too, at least *one* important love affair which left its mark on him. Weak lungs, fragile nerves, and constant heavy drinking took their toll on him, and after a breakdown in the autumn of 1908, followed by an eight-month stay at Dr. Daniel Jacobson's clinic in Copenhagen, Munch returned to Norway in the spring of 1909 and settled in the seaport town of Kragerø, on the Oslo fjord (Ill. p. 22).

Thus the wandering years came to an end; and although Munch in no sense turned his back on the outside world, from then on it was always to one of his various homes in Norway that he returned after traveling abroad.

The Kragerø years are dominated by Munch's work on the huge murals which cover the walls of the festival hall, the Aula, at Oslo University (figs. 128-131). For a time he also rented a large house on Jeløya, near Moss; bought a small property at Ramme, near Hvitsten, also close to the fjord; and in 1916 moved to the estate at Ekely, on the outskirts of Kristiania, as the city was then still called (Ill. p. 27). Here he continued a practice he had established at Kragerø, building large, open-air studios in the garden while confining himself to a spartan lifestyle in the main house. The household at most times comprised a gardener, a housekeeper, an indeterminate number of dogs, and an old white horse, Rousseau, which is featured in several of his paintings.

Munch became increasingly shy and withdrawn. The tendency was already evident during his first years at Ekely, although it would not be accurate to describe his life then as isolated; not until the 1920s and 1930s did the rumors of the solitary hermit begin to gain currency. The descriptions we have of his later life at Ekely present us finally with the picture of a man with limited social contacts, jealously guarding his privacy and pursuing a spartan lifestyle with regard to food, clothing, and his personal surroundings. From the many descriptions of Munch during these last years at Ekely, I choose one given by his friend, professor K. E. Schreiner, in the mid-1920s, and put into writing twenty years later:

"My pull at the bellrope at his gate acted as the signal for a terrific barking of dogs in the yard inside. Munch himself appeared and unlocked the gate, surrounded by two yapping, jumping setters. His first remark was: 'You arrive at a very suitable time, I have just emptied the lavatory bucket.' He employed no housekeeper at the time but looked after himself in order not to be disturbed in the house, as he said. From the balcony we entered his workroom. In it stood his easel, surrounded by palettes, paint tubes and brushes which were strewn about the floor. Watercolors and drawings in charcoal hung round about the walls. Prints were lying on the grand piano, on chairs and on the floor — dusty, creased, and partly torn. For one who had always considered these prints as sacred and unobtainable treasures, this treatment of them made a profound impression. From the workroom we went into his dining-cum-bedroom. In it was the bed with the red-striped bedcover and the radio next to it, the old clock and the wicker chair (Ill. p. 9 and fig. 164), paintings on the walls, drawings brutally stuck on the doors. An unusual and rank smell came from the kitchen — seeping out, as I later found, from the maid's room where his great St. Bernard dog, known from several of Munch's paintings, was imprisoned at the time. I was conducted round the garden and the studios. The impression was everywhere equally overwhelming . . . I remember from this my first visit in the studios that outside one of them one of the great sketches for the University festival hall decorations with a gaping hole in it was put up in one corner. I muttered words of regret; Munch: 'Yes, it is badly mutilated, just think of that dog, it bounced straight through the canvas.' I, naively: 'But how can you possibly let your pictures stay un protected like this?' Munch: 'My pictures only profit by being left out in the rain and the snow.' We walked back to the house, and Munch prepared a simple lunch consisting of his favorite brandy and milk biscuits. This menu became a standard for the first years and during my visits at Ekely. During the last years, when he had engaged a very proficient housekeeper, conditions were completely changed and the brandy was demoted from main course to dessert.''

This short summary of Munch's career suggests a division into three distinct periods:

The years 1880-1889 are spent in Kristiania, with short trips to Antwerp, Paris, and Copenhagen. The limited amount of formal training Munch had takes place during this period.

The years 1889-1909 are Munch's years of wandering.

He travels restlessly in Norway, France, and Germany, with occasional journeys to Italy, Switzerland, Austria, and Czechoslovakia. Between autumn 1889 and spring 1892 he is in France, where he again stays for lengthy periods in 1895-98 and in 1903. His career as a graphic artist begins in Berlin in 1894, where he takes up etching and lithography, continuing with woodcuts in Paris in 1896. His home base in Norway becomes Åsgårdstrand, where he buys himself a small house in 1897.

In the autumn of 1908 he has a breakdown in Copenhagen, spends eight months at Dr. Jacobson's clinic, and in May 1909 returns to Norway. He settles first at Kragerø, moves to Jeløya and Hvitsten, then in 1916 buys the Ekely property on the outskirts of Kristiania and establishes a permanent home there. Apart from isolated long journeys abroad after the first world war, he remains here until his death on January 23 1944.

Munch's work

Munch was 17 when he decided upon the direction his life should take. Throughout the following sixty-three years, until his death in January 1944, his calling as an artist dominated all his thoughts and was the focus of all his energy. His life's work comprises something like 1,700 canvases, a large number of sketches and drawings (many of them preliminary studies, but many also full-fledged works), and a sizable collection of prints. The graphic works alone comprise more than 800 different motifs, many of which, particularly among the woodcuts, survive as series of proof impressions, in different editions, and individually colored and adapted versions which, considered separately, often seem more like independent works of art than parts of a series of identical prints. Munch's creative vigor remained undiminished, even during those periods when one might imagine the pressures of a difficult and debilitating life would prove insurmountable. This is particularly true of the years between the turn of the century and his nervous breakdown of 1908. It is during precisely this time that we find him changing his entire mode of expression and laying the foundations for the direction his art would take in the latter part of his life.

There is obviously no place for a complete account of Munch's output in a short introduction such as this. Here our best guide to an understanding can perhaps be achieved by cutting a series of judicious sections at appropriate points through the great mass of available material. An outline of Munch's stylistic development and his understanding of form will provide an introductory overview; thereafter some observations on composition and use of formula in a few select paintings should also provide useful insight into the rest of them; while his thematic world may be examined from several different angles. Such an approach will, we hope, provide a combination of knowledge and understanding and should also convey some idea of the unity underlying Munch's works. Let us begin, therefore, by reviewing the way in which his style and form developed.

STYLE AND FORM: OUTLINE OF A DEVELOPMENT

The most dramatic changes in the development of style and form throughout Munch's long career as an artist coincide roughly with that division of his life into periods which we have suggested above. He matured early: even before his deci-

sion as a 17-year-old to dedicate his life to art, he had produced a series of exact and highly competent architectural studies, and by the summer of 1880 produced his first attempt in oils. To judge from the studies he made of the old Romanesque stone church as seen from the windows of his apartment in Grünerløkka in Oslo (figs. 1, 2, 3), he must have been a painstaking and conscientious worker. In a number of these drawings he seems to be conquering his subject stage by stage, so to speak. First, there is a preliminary sketch, in which he obviously captures something which he is reluctant to lose by overelaboration. This sketch is therefore put aside after being copied; the copy is then worked forward to a new stage. Sketch number two is then also copied and worked on until we reach number three. What must be considered the final results of this process are a number of oil sketches showing the main subject from different angles, although one would not like to hazard a guess as to which of these might be considered the final version (fig. 4).

The series devoted to Telthusbakken, which is the narrow road lined with small wooden houses which winds down the hill from the church, is executed with a sure compositional sense. Arne Eggum has suggested that motif was first attempted with the assistance of a camera lucida, something which seems likely given the very practical attitude towards drawing which characterized the military milieu in which Munch passed many of his summers. In letters from this period Munch mentions items of technical drawing equipment. Whatever the case, these small pictures already show the compositional sureness which typifies all of Munch's work. However, their old-fashioned, straightforward and slightly stylized realism was soon to give way to a far looser handling of detail, in which form and color are described in terms of their relationship to the lighting in the picture, and in which a certain emotive atmosphere is sought. Two paintings which he exhibited, *Early Morning* and *Morning* (fig. 10), from 1883 and 1884 respectively, are good examples of this; and the 1883 paintings, which show his aunt in her rocking chair and his father sitting at a coffee table (figs. 7, 9) typify his orientation towards a painterly formula which seems intended to create certain states of psychological moods in the observer.

These tendencies were therefore present in Munch's work even before his first trip abroad in the summer of 1885; but they were to achieve their fullest expression directly after.

The great collections in Antwerp, and later the Louvre, were accessible to him for immediate study, and a whole world of influences opened up to him: the Impressionists' splitting of colors, Rembrandt's chiaroscuro, Goya's expressivity, the sheer scale of the Velázquez portraits — we can see their effects on Munch immediately upon his return to Norway. At the Autumn Exhibition that year he showed a full-length portrait of his friend the painter Karl Jensen-Hjell (fig. 12), in an arrogant pose, with more than a touch of the insolent bohemian about him, the light reflected in his monocle suggested by a single white stroke. Few brushstrokes can have excited such a reaction among conservative art critics. Munch had clearly been looking at the portraits in the great collections, from Velázquez to Manet, probably assimilating something of the freer brushwork of Frans Hals or perhaps even of the contemporary Impressionists.

Another small group of pictures from this same period, the autumn and winter of 1885-86, among them studies for portraits of the painter's father, and the self-portrait from 1886 (fig. 15), are particularly worthy of attention. Most important of all, however, is *The Sick Child* (fig. 11). It marked a personal breakthrough in Munch's artistic development. He had struggled with the painting throughout the winter of 1885-86 before exhibiting it under the title *A Sketch* at the Autumn Exhibition in Kristiania in September 1886. The picture represents his sister Sophie, who died of tubercular consumption in 1877, at just 15 years of age.

Years later, in 1929, Munch himself was to write of this work:

"The first time I saw the sick child — the pale head with the red hair, striking against the white of the pillow — it made an impression on me which disappeared during the working process. The picture I produced on the canvas was good, but it was different. I made many changes in that painting in the course of the year — scraped it out — let it dissolve in the floating paint — and tried again and again to recapture that first impression — the translucent — pale skin against the canvas — the trembling mouth — the trembling hands.

I had stressed the chair with the glass too much, it distracted attention from the head. — When I looked at my painting I saw only the glass and the surroundings. — Should I take it all away? — No, its effect was to give depth and prominence to the head. — I scraped the surroundings half away, and left everything standing in abstract mass — one looked over the head and the glass.

I discovered also that my own eyelashes had played their part in contributing to the pictorial impression. — I suggested them therefore as shadows over the image. The head became in a way the picture. — Waves appeared in the picture — peripheries — with the head as their center. — I often made use of these waves later."

The Sick Child was exhibited prominently at the Autumn Exhibition, but was savaged by the critics. Few realized that in it a talented young painter had been struggling to achieve a formal language capable of conveying emotional weight of a kind unfamiliar to conventional contemporary painting — and unfamiliar to the avant-garde as well, since the Impressionists, until the appearance of van Gogh's later works, were chiefly interested in describing a visible, outer reality. Munch wanted to penetrate deeper than this and did so by investing his own personal sufferings and sorrows in his work.

Recalling his own memories of the work, Munch later wrote to his friend Jens Thiis that probably no other artist had ever "relived his subject-matter, to the last, painful drop in the cup, as I did with 'The Sick Child.' Because it wasn't just me sitting there, it was all of my loved ones too."

He had been searching for a new way of expressing personal feelings in paint. With its overworked, thick surface — the result of the painting being modelled, not merely brushed on — *The Sick Child* represents a clear breakthrough in Munch's artistic development; more than this, it is both technically and in its emotional implications a pioneering work in the development of modern European art.

If *The Sick Child* is a poem about Death, then two other works Munch painted at about the same time are based on bohemian ideas about Life: *Puberty* and *The Day After*. Both were done in 1886, and both are known to us only through later replicas (figs. 51, 53): the originals were destroyed by fire. One would like to have known more about the painterly qualities of these earlier versions, but we must content ourselves with remarking that both works clearly represented deeply felt personal and radical contributions to the world of contemporary European painting.

Perhaps in consequence of the harsh criticism Munch had met with, his work in the immediately succeeding years followed a line that was regarded in Kristiania as a rather more acceptable advanced type of naturalism, with reference points in the work of somewhat older Norwegian contemporaries such as Hans Heyerdahl and Munch's friend Christian Krohg. *The Net Mender*, painted during a sea trip to Hankø on the Oslo fjord in 1888, is a good example of this. Nevertheless, Munch remains exceptional in the degree to which he at times invests his paintings with a strong emotional content — as in *Evening*, again from 1888 (fig. 13), in which his sister Laura sits alone in the foreground, a rather stiff, staring expression on her face, while further back in the picture, two others handle the boat. What both paintings have in common is a firm grasp of the main lines of the composition — those clear lines of perspective which create the depth in the picture, and the definition of space in which the figures unfold.

Munch spent the spring and summer of 1889 in Kristiania and Åsgårdstrand before heading south in the beginning of October. Two important pictures had been completed in time for his large one-man show in the capital in April — the psychologically penetrating portrait of his friend, the leader of the bohemians Hans Jæger (fig. 16), and *Spring* (fig. 18), a sensitive but more conventional presentation of the same subject-matter that had caused such a furor over *The Sick Child* three years earlier. The decisive stylistic leap, however, came with the life-size portrait of his sister Inger sitting among the boulders on the beach at Åsgårdstrand. The family had rented a small fisherman's cottage, and in contemporary photographs we see the young painter at his easel, surrounded by members of his family as he paints a sketch of the stones in the portrait. In the painting he places his sister by the edge of the sea, against the sharply rising surface of the water, with no horizon, so that the whole scene is enclosed and concentrated on the central figure, painted in meditative harmony with the atmosphere in the stylized landscape of which she forms a part. Munch accentuates the outlines of things and suggests a flattening of shapes, mirroring a similar move towards a decorative painting style which was taking place in France at about the same time. The style would reappear in a more definite form in the painting of his friend Jappe Nilssen on the same beach at Åsgårdstrand, which he produced two years later under the title *Melancholy (Jappe on the Beach)* (fig. 28).

Yet his stylistic development did not proceed in clear and simple lines from *Inger on the Beach* to *Melancholy (Jappe on the Beach)*. When Munch travelled to Paris in October 1889, the metropolis was to provide him with his first experience of the real depth of modern French painting, and we see him experimenting with a new manner which he shortly afterwards abandons for experiments in yet another style.

Ingrid Langaard was the first to make a serious attempt to consider Munch's art in relation to developments in contemporary French art. Munch began fairly conventionally at Léon Bonnat's studio (fig. 14); Bonnat praised him, but Munch soon came to disagree with his teacher and moved to St. Cloud, where he produced impressionistic studies of the view across the river (fig. 20) as well as interiors featuring ordinary people from local drinking haunts (fig. 21). It is sometimes claimed that in these Munch was influenced by the folksy character-sketches of J. F. Raffaëlli, although Munch's works have a much more painterly quality.

It was at St. Cloud also that Munch formulated his famous manifesto, known to us in a version he produced in 1929, in which he put forward his proposals for a personal art that would depict "living human beings who breathe and feel, suffer and love. I felt that this was what I should do — it ought to be so easy — the flesh and blood would take shape, the colors live —."

Depressed by news of his father's death in late 1889, Munch brooded over memories of life at home and the loss of his mother, his sister, grandfather, and father: "And I am living with the dead . . . all the memories, the tiniest things, keep cropping up." He painted *Night in St. Cloud* (fig. 19), in which a dreaming figure seated by the illuminated window looking out over the Seine seems to crystallize the mood which quivers in the air of the ill-lit room. Not since *The Sick Child* (fig. 11), three years earlier, had Munch produced a painting of such psychological intensity. This time, however, the symbolic allusions were more obvious — the reflected cross on the floor suggests an image of death, and a profound melancholy is evoked by the contrast between the flow of color and life in the world outside the window and the brooding emptiness of the room surrounding the solitary male figure.

Paris in the spring of 1890 might have provided Munch with a fine opportunity to become acquainted with the new and exciting use of Symbolism in both literature and painting. It was already well on the way to acquiring the status of a movement. To judge by the pictures Munch painted back at home in Norway that summer, and later in Nice and Paris, he seems, however, to have been more interested in pursuing his studies of the masters of Impressionism and Pointillism. His small studies of views over the Seine have already been mentioned; the following spring at Nice he produced several paintings built over the same compositional pattern, so to speak, in which architectural forms provide the solid base for the reproduction of light and atmosphere in the manner of the Impressionists. The technique is utilized most completely in the large painting of Karl Johans gate in Kristiania on a spring day, executed with more than a touch of pointillist influence (fig. 22), and in two street studies from Paris (*Rue Lafayette* and *Rue de Rivoli*) done in May of the following year (figs. 24, 25).

It was probably at some point during the spring of 1891 that Munch became fully aware of what were soon to be the dominant tendencies in French art. An interest in decorative surface and expressive line was now replacing the pictorial language of Impressionism, with its suffusions of light rendered in characteristic sketchy brushwork. Color was no longer to be used to describe a visible reality but on the contrary to convey the *felt* reality of the inner world. Theories were advanced about a language of color in which certain colors corresponded not only to certain distinct human emotions but also to particular notes in music. This in turn led to the conception of paintings as a mode of psychological expression. Artists moved away from the depiction of the outer, physical world and turned inward, in an attempt to describe the secret life of the mind and heart.

Those few short weeks in Paris in the spring of 1891 undoubtedly provided Munch with decisive insights into the new art, and led to a major personal breakthrough for him later that summer. Now he found a quite new and wholly personal style, capable of containing the kind of psychological intensity which he had previously tried to express in *The Sick Child* and *Night in St. Cloud*. The single painting which is the key to the whole of his production throughout the Symbolist 1890s was executed during that summer in Åsgårdstrand. We know it in five different versions, painted over the years under the title of *Jappe on the Beach* or *Melancholy* (fig. 28). *Melancholy* is the direct outcome of the movement centered on Paul Gauguin and the so-called Nabis — a group of young artists which started in Paris towards the end of the 1880s, with Maurice Denis as its foremost theoretician and advocate of the principle of expressive simplification. Other, related influences played a part, and the full background for the dramatic new direction Munch's art took in the summer of 1891 and the years immediately thereafter should include his studies of the later, expressionist works by van Gogh, the drastic handling of composition in works by Degas and Toulouse-Lautrec, and in the emphasis on surface and line supported by an expressive use of color in Gauguin's paintings. Munch must have studied all of these artists, as well as others who were of value to him, during his visits to Paris between 1889 and 1891, but perhaps most particularly during the month preceding his return to Norway on May 29 1891, a month in which Symbolism was strikingly well represented at art exhibitions and in the city's cultural life in general.

Melancholy, done in the summer of 1891, was followed by a small group of interesting studies of the Casino at Monte Carlo which Munch executed in Nice. As Arne Eggum points out, the milieu surrounding the roulette tables at Monte Carlo must have been a veritable gold mine for Munch in his studies of people in extreme psychological states. We know from his journals how he reacted to the scene, and the painting *By the Roulette* (fig. 35) demonstrates his mastery of the engulfing perspective, with those almost faceless forms standing round the table. These are arranged in a dramatic but controlled disquiet; a loose, almost untidy brushwork heightens the feeling of psychological tension. The colors, too, add to the tension — details in angry red contrast with the green of the lamp, and the felt table surface. If *Melancholy* established the direction of Munch's symbolist art of the 1890s, *By the Roulette* pointed ahead to his next great stylistic breakthrough, after the turn of the century. Along with the impressionist works done in St. Cloud, the pictures done in Nice and the street scenes of Paris, these two works demonstrate Munch's ability to extract the pictorial elements which, through an active creative process, then became a part of his own highly personal artistic language.

Roughly speaking, one can say that Munch's work up to 1900 is based on the studies that went into *Melancholy* (*Jappe on the Beach*) and the Monte Carlo paintings. Furthermore, it seems likely that sketches for many of the most important works of the 1890s existed as early as autumn 1891 and spring 1892. This applies to such central motifs as *Vampire* (fig. 44), *The Voice* (fig. 43), *Moonlight on the Shore* (fig. 33), *The Storm* (fig. 38), and above all *Despair* (fig. 29), which was to develop through various stages into the epoch-making *The Scream* of 1893 (fig. 39).

All these paintings belong to the series which Munch grouped together in the 1890s under the general title *The*

Frieze of Life. They marked his attempt to describe the most powerful forces in the life of an individual: lust, love, angst, and death. The series probably never comprised an exact number of specific paintings, but was shown in its most complete form at the large Secessionist Exhibition in Berlin in 1902, at which Munch exhibited by invitation. Here his paintings were arranged in representative groupings and were praised by the critics. *The Frieze of Life* is a central part of Munch's works and will be discussed in more detail later on.

The formal language which Munch mastered during his years in France, and which also characterized his contribution to the Berlin exhibition in 1902, dissolved during the ensuing years under the pressure of new forces moving both within and without him. A new kind of expressionism makes its appearance, in which the paintings are built up of what often look like careless and almost haphazard brushstrokes — yet they are always based on a firm underlying composition. The change can be detected in *Golgotha*, done in 1900 (fig. 81), and even more clearly in a splendid little landscape of 1903 (fig. 89). The new style is also distinctly present in the landscapes painted in the summer of 1904, which were intended as a frieze for the children's bedroom in Max Linde's house in Lübeck (fig. 97).

A clear and definitive stylistic break did not occur, however, until the summer of 1907, when Munch was staying at Warnemünde, on the Baltic Sea, and, by his own account, experienced a need to change his style of painting. He himself mentions experiments he conducted in the use of broad, meter-long brushstrokes, remarking that "a certain pre-cubism expressed itself" through this particular way of breaking up the surface of the canvas. Every bit as striking is the freer expressionism which comes to light in the series called *The Green Room* (figs. 112, 113) and in the portrait *Old Man in Warnemünde* (fig. 108) — powerful brushstrokes apparently dashed down, and contours outlined in thick stripes of color laid onto the canvas directly from the tube. If we take into account the most notable work of that summer, the tryptych *Bathing Men* (fig. 115), an even richer and more complex picture of Munch's development emerges. Here we find a carefully considered use of short, choppy, slanting brushstrokes to build up the central area into a richly colored celebration of masculine power and strength in a natural setting by the sea, the origin and source of all life on earth.

The works referred to here also demonstrate the way in which Munch could work in several different personal styles at the same time — much as he did during the experimental years around 1890. But viewed as a whole, the products of that summer finally achieve the long-heralded break with the decorative surface-style of the 1890s. Now the ground was prepared for a free and personal painterly expression which would characterize Munch's work from now until the last years of his life. The great murals for the main hall at Oslo University, which occupied him between 1909 and 1916, obviously demanded a monumental, decorative approach, and in *Self-portrait after the Spanish Flu* from 1919 (fig. 148) he returns to an older, linear style of composition which recalls Whistler's portrait of Thomas Carlyle. But such diversity does not lessen the impression of free-flowing imaginative inventiveness which characterizes that very important part of Munch's œuvre created after 1907. No comprehensive characterization can give an adequate account of this period, but some of the most important works may be mentioned in order to underscore its richness. One is a firmly constructed forest interior done in 1911-12, in which a yellow log surges forward in a kind of contrapuntal contrast to the depth of

perspective in the painting (fig. 126); in another, *The Murderer*, done in 1910 (fig. 125), a ghostly figure with guiltily dangling hands walks out of a lushly colored landscape towards the spectator. Then there is the female nude weeping in despair against a fierce red background in which the color, thinned by turpentine, flows almost like watercolor (fig. 134); the attempts to capture movement in the legs of the advancing workers in the monumental *Workers on Their Way Home* of 1913-15 (fig. 136); or the reflection of emotional turbulence conveyed by the disordered bedclothes in *Model by the Wicker Chair* of 1919-21 (fig. 149). If we consider these along with the wonderfully restrained portrait of the model Birgit Prestøe on the sofa, done in the classical 1920s (fig. 153), the contrast provides us with some idea of the sheer richness and variety of Munch's later work. This is the work of a colorist, a painter, the creation of a master sufficiently sure of himself to work with an apparent spontaneity that is impulsive and rich but always rooted in a firm sense of basic compositional form.

COMPOSITION AND USE OF FORMULA

Quite often I have gone down into the basement of the Munch Museum and picked out a painting — an unfinished work, perhaps, or some sketch that appears to have been rattled off — to hang on the wall of my office, hoping to enter into it by daily contact. Invariably I am gripped by a strength in these pictures and sense the unity underlying all the different elements of the painting — Edvard Munch's sure and powerful compositional sense.

I am by no means sure how he set about achieving this. As we have seen, he may have made use in his youth of technical devices such as the camera obscura and the camera lucida, but there is no evidence of their use in the works of his maturity. Here and there one sees thin guidelines in a sketch or drawn on the canvas — a drawing of his dogs enclosed within a triangular figure; or a composition depicting figures in violent movement which is enclosed within a parallelogram. For the large canvases which were stretched to take the enlargements of sketches done for the murals in the University's main hall, he obviously used the familiar grid-system, but his work generally bears little trace of the conscious use of technical devices; no measurements for the golden section, no complicated geometrical delineations underneath the paint, propping up the visible imagery.

This might be related to an ability to mentally visualize which one is tempted to ascribe to him. We know that his uncle, P. A. Munch, had a photographic memory for words and sentences such as that Mozart had for music. Indeed, it is said of P. A. Munch that he was afraid to read railway timetables because it was so difficult for him to get the figures out of his mind afterwards.

Numerous anecdotes indicate that Edvard Munch possessed this ability to memorize and to "paint in his head." Ludvig Ravensberg tells of how he visited Munch at Kragerø one morning: The painter was standing in front of a large canvas. He waved his brush a couple of times, made a couple of marks on the canvas, then suggested that they go for a walk. Munch then remarked that Ravensberg must suppose that he didn't work much — but that this would be wrong. "I work all the time. I'm working now, while we're walking." In light of this observation, Munch's many claims to the effect that "I don't paint what I see, but what I saw" acquire a new meaning: he probably wrestled with his thematic material in his imagination, as well as in the many preliminary sketches for finished works which we are able to study. He was able, in a sense, to paint with his thoughts; and when the interior, ideal picture was completed, one might imagine that the realization of it in paint was a comparatively rapid process, having every appearance of effortless facility to those unacquainted with the struggles that lay behind it.

Such a working method must have accentuated that tendency towards simplification and concentration on the chief effects which we remark early on in Munch's work: the paring down of detail in *The Sick Child* (fig. 11), in order to focus attention on the clasped hands and the face of the dying girl; and later, when Munch in the 1890s became one of the leading synthesists, a general simplification of forms into surfaces and a play of lines. As we have seen, Munch abandoned this kind of decorative simplification after 1900, but his appreciation of the need for a firm underlying structure remained.

Within a structural framework such as this we are able to look more closely at a number of characteristic compositional techniques which always serve to stress the psychological content of the pictures. One of these is the use of an exaggeratedly strong perspective. We see intimations of this in a pair of landscapes painted in the warm and apparently carefree summers of 1888 and 1890 — *The Net Mender* and *Arrival of the Mail Boat* (fig. 23). It is usual to refer to the influence of Krohg and Heyerdahl in these paintings, but well worthy of comment is the hint of drama suggested by the play of lines in the view of the quay on the left-hand side of both paintings, the way in which it seems to hurry away into the background. The classic example of reinforced perspective is to be found, of course, in *The Scream* of 1893 (fig. 39), in which the bridge disappears on its way inward towards the two friends walking away from us into the painting. The perspective heightens the sense of claustrophobic distress which surrounds the main figure. The same effect crops up in numerous different contexts in Munch's later work too. In *The Yellow Log* of 1911-12 (fig. 126), perspective acquires a doubled strength, in one direction opening inwards towards the tree-trunks in the wood, while the yellow log itself, seeming to hurtle forward out of the picture, opposes the invitation inwards. *Spring Plowing* of 1916 (fig. 144) is one of a group of pictures in which this technique is used, and we can study it at its most dramatic in *Galloping Horse* (fig. 127). Through the use of exaggerated perspective and related compositional techniques, Munch is able to create a sense of dynamic space, a kind of tension in a state of equilibrium which remains unresolved, but which always functions to create a remarkable intensity. One might imagine that it reflects a corresponding unresolved tension in his own mind.

At other times Munch would use other effects to express different psychological attitudes. In *Workers on Their Way Home*, done in 1913-15 (fig. 136), the stream of advancing men seems about to spill out of the frame as though to take possession of the observer's space. The picture has been interpreted by some as depicting the triumphant advance of the working class; but in fact the composition seems to suggest a disturbing disharmony, clearly evident in the faces and postures of the three main figures at the front of the canvas, on the left; the central figures in *Bathing Men* (fig. 115), on the other hand, are resolved with full plastic weight in a composition characterized by horizontal lines, which give an air of calm and stability to the self-aware, powerful male figures advancing towards us in the brilliant sunlight.

Besides the use of exaggerated perspective and similar techniques in Munch's compositional repertoire, we can study

the way in which he directs his characters with a sure grasp of psychological effect. One example is his use of a central figure, often in situations in which the other figures in the composition seem isolated, both from each other and from the observer, so that the central figure affords the only opportunity of emotional contact with the observer. The little girl screaming in fear and confusion at the sight of her dead mother is one example (fig. 75), and her rôle as the agent of the emotional message is reinforced by the color of her dress — a characteristic red. Another important instance occurs in *Death in the Sickroom* (fig. 56), in which Edvard's sister Inger is presented to us full-face, as a tragic mask, and the youngest sister, Laura, sits hunched in the foreground, immersed in her own grief. The shrunken, introverted pose of this figure was one Munch used often: we recognize it in *Ashes* (fig. 48), for example, as well as in other compositions.

The third figure in the foreground of the painting is that of Munch himself. Half turning from us, he compels our gaze into the right-hand background of the picture, where the real drama is taking place, with death invisibly present among the group of figures gathered around the dying girl's chair.

Thus, in *Death in the Sickroom*, our attention is first attracted by the dominant grouping in the foreground and thereafter swiftly transferred to a less dominating group further into the painting where, as it transpires, the real import of the scene resides. Something similar happens in *Red Virginia Creeper* (fig. 78), in which the apparent agitation of the man in the foreground reflects a threatening emotional atmosphere associated with the house in the background, conveyed partly through the wide-open windows, but even more effectively via the fiery red of the Virginia creeper climbing up the walls of the house. In *Jealousy* (figs. 61, 62), a major element in *The Frieze of Life*, the situation seems clear enough: the face in the foreground is that of Stanislaw Przybyszewski, and the standing figure in the background resembles Munch himself. The woman stands, like Eve, in an attitude of temptation, naked beneath a dress which is open all the way down the front, and once again we encounter the use of a fiery red to illustrate a situation charged with emotional intensity. In *Melancholy (Jappe on the Beach)* (fig. 28), Munch's major work from 1891, the origins of Jappe Nilssen's despair are to be found in the figures on the quay far back in the depths of the painting, where the man with the oars accompanies Jappe's beloved and his rival.

In the light of these pictures we have described here, in which our interpretation of the compositional technique seems fairly obvious, it is tempting to read another meaning into the composition Munch chose for his *Self-portrait in Weimar* (fig. 106) of 1906. Here Munch himself stands out in the foreground, personifying the atmosphere in the picture. A patch of passionate red marking an open fireplace resembles an aura behind his head, while the perspective sways inwards between the rows of tables in the restaurant. If we look carefully at the picture, we soon notice a second space, opening on the right, which claims our attention equally. Here we focus on a small, isolated figure clad in black and without discernible facial features. The feeling of unease suggested by this figure grows until it seems as though the depressive atmosphere surrounding the foreground figure might originate here. If this is the case, the small figure must carry symbolic weight: it might be Death itself, or the embodiment of the oppressive burden of grief and depression which Munch's depiction of himself in the foreground clearly conveys.

Another fascinating study is Munch's use of psychologically loaded images from the early 1890s onwards. The large, doom-laden shadow is one of these. We see it thrown on the wall behind the portrait of himself sitting in a dejected attitude in front of his fireplace, most likely drawn in St. Cloud in the winter of 1891 (fig. 27); and find it again as a whole sackful of dark intimations in *Puberty* from 1894 (fig. 51). *Rose and Amélie* of 1893 (fig. 40), Munch's painting of two whores, uses shadows to convey the dark and threatening nature of the erotic life which these two "ladies" represent. The use of a heavy, dark shadow with its own independent emotional effect is seen chiefly in the works of the 1890s, although we find it used as an aid to psychological expression as late as 1907, in the large version of *The Death of Marat* (fig. 114), where it heightens the sinister atmosphere surrounding the erect female figure.

If the shadow is something born of Munch's own painterly intuition, the use of expressively reinforced lines is a device found in many of his symbolic pictures from the 1890s. According to Munch himself, he used it for the first time in *The Sick Child* of 1885-86 (fig. 11). It seems just as likely that the motif has its origins in Munch's interest in psychological magnetism and related irrational phenomena which we know preoccupied him, and which probably took a turn for the stronger about the time of his meeting with August Strindberg and the circle of German intellectuals in Berlin. From this time onwards we find linear forms in both his portraits and in other works which resemble more than anything else the force lines in a magnetic field. Around the head of Dagny Juel, in the superb full-length portrait in blue of 1893 (fig. 36), we can see, even in reproduction, a framework of concentric lines probably intended to represent spreading waves, much as early representations of radio waves showed them radiating from the tops of radio masts. We find similar circles in the portrait of the mystic Albert Kollmann (fig. 88); and in his lithographic portrait of Strindberg done in 1896 (fig. 64) Munch placed a female figure in the frame. According to contemporary occult theory, the play of lines formed by the extension of her mane of hair can be divided into the gentle and organically flowing feminine principle on the right-hand side, and the energetic, active zigzag of the masculine principle on the left. Interpreted thus, the wavelike lines round the Madonna-figure of 1893 acquire a new meaning, as do the multiple contour lines used as early as 1897 in *The Kiss* (fig. 74), and most markedly in the woodcuts of 1897-98 (figs. 72, 73), which render visible the emotional intensity of the motifs. These observations are drawn from Arne Eggum's stimulating treatment of the subject in his book *Munch and Photography*.

The question of Munch's attitude towards faith and a philosophy of life will be touched upon later; but the question arises also with regard to Munch's use of certain formulaic elements in his pictorial world. Consider, for example, his use of the tree. In pictures like *Metabolism* (fig. 79), *Eye in Eye* (fig. 52), *Fertility I* (fig. 77), and *Adam and Eve*, a man and a woman are depicted on either side of a tree trunk. They are individuals in the long line of generations carrying forward the life-cycle represented by the tree. In *Metabolism*, a fetus drawn within the trunk of the tree was later painted over. And in one of the university murals, *Alma Mater* (fig. 130), the outlines of a child's face can be discerned high up in the trunk of the large pine tree to the right of the central figure. Both *Fertility* and *Eye in Eye* feature a large, sawn-off branch colored in such a way as to draw one's attention to it. One suspects here a symbolic meaning from Munch's private mythology, although it is not possible to say precisely what that meaning might be.

The tree symbol is more accessible when it is presented as the chain of life itself in such fundamental natural processes as metamorphosis or photosynthesis: *Metabolism* was

the title Munch gave his paraphrase of the theme of Adam and Eve from 1899 (fig. 79). We see the tree's roots drawing nourishment from rotting organic matter, and in the frame, above the top of the tree, Munch has introduced a number of images associated with Kristiania — Akershus Castle, Our Savior's Church — to symbolize the pulsating life of city-dwelling human beings. The motif persists, with variations, through the years: in one such, fertile Woman stands beneath the crown of the tree and above an earth pregnant with skeletons, the whole scene illuminated by the life-giving rays of the sun (fig. 145). During the first world war he also took comfort in the motif, in a lithograph done in 1915 which shows a tree growing from a heap of corpses, as symbol and promise of the continuity of life on earth (fig. 146).

In all of these instances we see that the tree motif is ascribed meaning as a sign, with a more or less specific function which Munch utilizes in a wide variety of contexts. One might almost see it as a hieroglyph, something from the artist's private world of iconography, the precise meaning of which is not always accessible to us. *The Flower of Pain* (fig. 71) is another such hieroglyph, its meaning most clearly grasped when it grows nourished by the blood of the artist's own heart, as in this drawing done in 1897. The flower occurs again in *Woman in Three Stages* (fig. 47), calm and passionate beside the dejected male figure on the right. In *Eye in Eye* (fig. 52) it grows behind the man's back; might the intention here be to express the growth of creative power through spiritual suffering? A quality opposed by the little dollhouse to the left behind the woman, symbolizing perhaps the closed life of the family under the domination of the woman, an environment in which, according to Munch, the creative instincts of the male intellect could not thrive.

Still another hieroglyph, related to the magnetic force-fields, is that of flowing female hair. Two lyrical extracts from *The Tree of Knowledge* will illustrate this: "When you sailed away over the sea and left me, it was as though we were still bound to one another by fine threads that sawed as though across an open wound"; and "When we stood and looked at one another, and your eyes looked into mine, I felt as though invisible threads passed from your eyes into mine, binding our hearts together." The quotations relate directly to a number of motifs in which the woman's hair, almost like electrical wire, reaches out for the man and traps him (figs. 45, 52, 62, 69).

Other hieroglyphs are more problematic. The bearded face of an aged man crops up in several places — in the extreme left of the drawing *Beneath the Yoke* (fig. 68), for example, and in the foreground of *Golgotha* (fig. 81). The figure resembles both Christian Krohg and Munch's own father, and may represent a kind of dominating father/teacher figure whose precise importance eludes us.

One atmospheric element which is easier to interpret crops up for the first time in the early 1890s and reappears in Munch's paintings of shorelines in the 1900s. We find it in a number of the major works in *The Frieze of Life*, in the woodcuts *The Lonely Ones* (fig. 76) and *Separation* (fig. 45), and most notably in *The Dance of Life* (fig. 80). All of these feature a golden full moon, large and round, close to the horizon and casting a columnar reflection over the sea, a reflection which widens at one end as it lifts towards the moon itself, and which breaks in the faint waves that reach the shore. The motif is used in nature scenes with a strongly erotic atmosphere, and must undoubtedly be considered a phallic symbol. Maybe this private hieroglyph has long historical antecedents — one thinks of the Egyptian ankh sign which combines masculine and feminine in a single divine symbol.

MUNCH'S MOTIFS

Edvard Munch's thematic world is deeply and consistently rooted in his own personal experiences — the people he met, his surroundings, his own intense emotional life. His travels at home and abroad in Europe can be traced through his paintings, and his work is autobiographical to an unusual degree. I shall make a few points here about the realism that lies behind it all, in spite of formal abstractionism, and also draw attention to a few particularly noteworthy thematic groupings.

Everyday reality

Although Munch was one of the great innovators within the Symbolist movement that influenced most European art in the 1890s, one finds a surprising degree of fidelity to everyday realism in his depictions of the great moving forces of life. He rarely created a whole new reality, preferring to let the spiritual content of the painting emerge against a background of places and objects near and dear to him. Even in a highly abstract work like *The Scream* (fig. 39) of 1893, the hills around the Kristiania fjord are reproduced with a proportional exactness within the flowing outlines of the landscape surrounding the surface of the water. The isthmus projecting from the right in the center of the painting is a representation of the headland upon which King Haakon V Magnusson built Akershus Castle around 1300. Further to the right, the dome hinted at in several treatments of the motif is that of the neo-Gothic Church of the Holy Trinity. The entire landscape is seen in fact from a position below Ekeberg, to the east of the city, which can be located with some degree of precision even today.

Such fidelity to one's surroundings was quite in keeping with the prevailing naturalism of the 1880s, and the fact that Munch painted views from Kristiania and its surroundings, interiors peopled by his brothers and sister, his father and other relatives, or portraits of artist friends, comes as no surprise to us. *The Sick Child* (fig. 11), his great breakthrough painting of winter 1885-86, was done in the family's apartment. The chair in which the dying girl sat is today the property of the Munch Museum. And when Munch, towards the end of the 1880s, traveled the coast on those summer excursions of his, he painted landscapes from Vrengen, Hankø, and, later, from his beloved Åsgårdstrand. The rocky beach there provides a realistic background in the portrait of his sister Inger done in 1889, and the actual coastline curves exactly as we see it do in *Melancholy* (fig. 28).

This fidelity to *place* persisted throughout Munch's life. Only on very rare occasions did he create imaginary scenes, along the lines, say, of Odilon Redon, or Gustave Moreau. His real landscapes invariably possess an abstract quality, and once in a while combine several different elements to form a new whole, as in *Angst*. Here we find the landscape of *The Scream* (fig. 39) combined with the advancing tide of pale human faces from *Evening on Karl Johan Street* (fig. 34). Usually, however, Munch put parts of some familiar landscape directly into his paintings, whether these were works with a literary character, like *The Voice* (fig. 43) or *Woman in Three Stages* (fig. 47), or purely physically descriptive, as in the street scenes from Paris, the beach at Nice, the moody views of the landscape round Nordstrand in Oslo from 1900, or places seen in northern Germany, Kragerø, Hvitsten, Moss, or Ekely.

This sense of everyday reality is heightened in a sense by the way in which Munch so often makes a personal appearance in his paintings, a fact which again emphasizes just how autobiographical an artist he was. We seem to recognize him as the client in a whorehouse, more or less disguised (fig. 41), driven on by lust, bowed down by shame; as the creative and suffering artist in various allegories (fig. 71); as a central figure in *The Dance of Life* (fig 80) and *Golgotha* (fig. 81); in a number of erotic works — with Tulla Larsen in *Man and Woman* (fig. 103), with an anonymous model in *The Bite* (fig. 138); as a tragically self-descriptive Osvald in a sketch for Ibsen's *Ghosts* (fig. 154), or with self-derision, as the aging *Peer Gynt* (fig. 139). The group of erotic paintings with a model done in Ekely (ca. 1915-21), and the bohemian paintings of the late 1920s, bring the series of appearances to a close. In addition, we have the overt self-portraits which flowed from brush, pen, and pencil throughout his long life. Munch was the kind of artist who constantly held up a mirror for self-observation, and who depicted himself in relation to Woman, to Art, to Life, and to Death.

Alternative versions

When Munch, while still very young, painted the old church above the row of small houses along Telthusbakken in Oslo, his carefully executed study formed the basis of several "final" versions, in the form of small oil paintings in which the subject is studied from slightly different viewpoints and with variant use of color. Thus this little series points forward to a working method that was to be characteristic of the mature Munch. Time and again we find him investigating a particular theme through a number of versions, all of which resemble one another quite closely, and many of which, it would seem, have equal status in his eyes. At times it is legitimate to speak of preliminary sketches which form the basis of a more impressive finished work — the two early versions of *The Death of Marat* or *The Murderess* (figs. 105, 107) are good examples of this, although both have considerable value as works in their own right. At other times it is more difficult to distinguish between the preparation and the completion: Munch painted eighteen versions of *The Girls on the Bridge* (figs. 87, 94, 95, 161), and it would be more accurate to describe them as variants rather than as a developing series. Additionally, the quality is maintained throughout most of the eighteen versions. The motif was also essayed as a woodcut. Among the most frequent repetitions we find some of the central motifs from *The Frieze of Life* — Munch returned frequently to *Madonna* (fig. 54), *The Scream* (fig. 39), *Vampire* (fig. 44), *Woman in Three Stages* (fig. 47) and *The Dance of Life* (fig. 80). *The Sick Child* (fig. 11), his breakthrough work from the winter of 1885-86, is known to us in five later versions, one stemming, as far as we can make out, from 1896, two from 1907, one from 1921-22, and one probably from 1927. Referring to this, Munch wrote to his friend Jens Thiis that "they're all making such a fuss about the fact that I'm painting the same thing several different times — but a picture and a motif I have struggled with for a whole year cannot be said to be finished in one painting."

We can suggest many practical reasons for the fact that certain motifs were repeated in this fashion. The same theme may have been recreated for several different collectors, for example. We know also that Munch did not like being parted from his paintings. When one was sold he would often paint a new version for his own collection. Commissioned portraits were often produced in two versions, with the sitter himself choosing the one he wanted, and Munch keeping the other. These alternative versions represented different aspects of his artistic thinking about a single motif. From at least the time when he settled permanently in Norway, he lived with his work, constantly rearranging it around himself and often adding to a painting long after its original creation. His paintings were the world of his thoughts, in much the same way that a scholar's books form his intellectual universe.

Motifs which were repeated after an interval of years often changed in character. At times the difference might involve the appearance of a new meaning in a painting, as in the 1902 version of *Fertility II* (fig. 91), in which the youthful couple of the 1898 version are depicted as aged, the old man holding a scythe — the symbol of death — instead of the stick the young man holds in the earlier version. Something similar occurs in *By the Deathbed (Fever)*. The masks on the wall in the background of the 1893 version (fig. 37) disappear in the large new version of 1915 (fig. 140), and are replaced by a patterned wallpaper. The wall at the foot of the bed, however, seems to provide a source of light for the whole painting.

Where Munch employs an entirely new color scheme, the changes can be dramatic, as in the last versions of *The Ladies on the Bridge* (fig. 161) and *The Lonely Ones* (fig. 160) — both perhaps inspired by the large exhibition of German Expressionist painters which visited Oslo in 1932.

Interesting changes in the character of the motifs also occur where a change of medium is involved. When in 1894 Munch began his graphic work, he immediately recreated a number of his most important works, particularly from *The Frieze of Life*, as etchings, lithographs, and later as woodcuts. Here the motifs often acquire a new, concentrated power, while the unusual qualities of the new media also contributed to alter the character of the original creations (figs. 57, 60, 62, 66, 67, 72, 73, 76).

We find the same fondness for repeated descriptions of scenes, and variations and adaptations of sequences of events, in Munch's posthumous papers. These contain a number of autobiographical accounts treated in this fashion. His love affair with Tulla Larsen from 1898 to 1902 features strongly. Here we find alternative descriptions of events in which the central facts remain unaltered while details and narrative standpoint change from one description to the next. This intense concentration on the same material over long periods of time is one of the psychological fundamentals in Munch's attitude towards his motifs.

Friezes, series, decorative works

The first we hear of Munch working on a series of pictures is in a letter to the Danish painter Johan Rohde in the spring of 1893, in which he mentions that he is currently engaged in studies "for a series of pictures — to which most of my pictures . . . belong — e.g. the man and the woman by the sea — the red air (*Anxiety*) — the picture with the swan — these, which were a bit difficult to understand — when they're all put together — should be easier to understand — it's about love and death." At an exhibition in Berlin later in the same year he showed a series of six paintings under the title *Love*. He used the same title again when the series, expanded to include fourteen paintings, was again exhibited at Berlin in 1895. The most famous presentation of *The Frieze of Life* was at Berlin in 1902, where twenty-two paintings decorated the large entry hall at the Secessionist exhibition, this time under the title *From the Life of the Modern Soul*. The title *The Frieze of Life* occurs in a manuscript in Munch's hand which can probably be dated to about 1902-10. He writes of "the large frieze, the Frieze of Life, which . . . is intended

to depict the circle of life — the beginnings of love — the dance of life — love at its height, its decline, its death —." When he exhibited the frieze in Kristiania in 1918, he described the pictures in the exhibition catalogue. "I have worked on this frieze, at long intervals, for about thirty years" he wrote. Among the earlier works he mentions *The Kiss* (fig. 55), *Melancholy* (fig. 28), *Hands* (fig. 42), *Anxiety* from 1890-91 and *Vampire* (fig. 44), *The Scream* (fig. 39) and *Madonna* (fig. 54) from the following year (but illustrated here partly in later versions), and describes the frieze as "a series of decorative paintings which, together, are supposed to give a picture of life . . . a poem about life, love and death."

The frieze developed through the 1890s into a rich triad built around the themes of love, angst, and death — all described in that decoratively expressive style Munch had developed in *Melancholy (Jappe on the Beach)* (fig. 28), painted at Åsgårdstrand in the summer of 1891. With this picture he had discovered how to simplify the complex world of mental impressions into a pictorial language with both universal reference and emotional content. "Soul-painting" was one expression used by Munch's contemporaries to describe an art which attempts to depict the great, moving forces in human life — as Munch the artist experienced them.

Foremost among these forces is eroticism, described in terms of the violent emotional upheavals that occur when man and woman come together. Munch paints woman alone, captive of a mood which permeates the nature she is part of, in the dimness between the trees against a dark night sea across which moonlight shines in a phallic column of light which gives the picture its erotic atmosphere (*The Voice*, fig. 43); he paints her as one of a couple, lost in each other's gaze, blushing and warm, borne on a passion which has its origins outside herself, the man pale and obviously lost in the encounter (*Eye in Eye*, fig. 52); the theme gets a new interpretation in *Attraction* (fig. 69), in which her hair twines around his neck, holding him close to her as though an electric current had passed between them. Later comes the pain — consummation, separation, despair (*Vampire*, fig. 44; *Madonna*, fig. 54; *Separation*, fig. 45; *The Scream*, fig. 39), along with other motifs depicting the complications which arise to prevent the harmonious development of the erotic relationship, and which, in Munch's world, always underline the man's loneliness and psychological isolation, as in *Melancholy (Jappe on the Beach)* (fig. 28), *Jealousy* (fig. 61), and *Ashes* (fig. 48). In most of these paintings the woman appears as the enraptured one, borne along by great passion, a being in thrall to the great mystery of life; but now and then she is the victor, the hard one. *Woman in Three Stages* (fig. 47) from 1894, represents Munch's theory of the threefold nature of Woman: "the dreaming woman — the woman possessed by the joy of life — and Woman as the nun, the pale figure standing behind the trees," as he explained to Henrik Ibsen when the two met in 1895. Turning away from them all is the man — pale, eyes closed in anguish, and with the blood-red flower of pain growing at his feet — victim of the capricious play of powers beyond all human control.

One automatically uses a heightened prose-style in trying to describe *The Frieze of Life*. Munch was affected the same way himself, and his attempts to explain its motifs in words are really prose-poems, of considerable merit in themselves. They provide the key to understanding a way of thinking which was characteristic of its time as well as highly personal. From Munch's own letters we know that he had planned to publish a collection of texts and pictures, in which these "notes from the diary of my soul" would accompany his painting, so that, "arm in arm, in a single work, pictures and printed works would be united," as he wrote to the Swedish art historian Ragnar Hoppe in 1929.

These notes are numerous, and are found in sketchbooks, notebooks, letters, and manuscripts in the archives of the Munch Museum. They cover the whole of his life as a painter, although many of the most important (from our point of view) undoubtedly date from the beginning of the 1890s if not even earlier.

Munch worked on the organization of this material several times in his life. At the large 1978 exhibition of his work at the National Gallery in Washington, D.C., a series of prints pasted on sheets of thin cardboard was displayed. They were described by Bente Torjusen in the catalogue as a series known to us from contemporary sources. Clearly Munch had worked on these during his 1896-97 stay in Paris with the intention of publishing them in a limited edition under the title *The Mirror*. The series was exhibited in twenty-five parts in Kristiania in 1897. It is particularly interesting in that it shows that five years before its major presentation in Berlin in 1902, *The Frieze of Life* had already attained its full dimensions. We do not know what happened to the Washington prints immediately after the exhibition, but they later reappeared in a private collection in Norway and are now housed at the Busch-Reisinger Museum in Cambridge, Massachusetts.

There were no texts directly related to the prints in the *Mirror* series, but the Munch Museum has a large book of cuttings which was also exhibited in Washington, accompanied by an article in the catalog by Gerd Woll, curator of graphics at the museum. Here Munch has sometimes drawn directly on the pages of the book, sometimes pasted in prints and drawings, and sometimes simply inserted loose sheets of artwork, accompanied by texts written in his own hand, using capital letters and a variety of colors (fig. 110). The relationship between words and pictures is fairly clear, and thus also Munch's own interpretations of the paintings. The large book of cuttings bears the title *The Tree of Knowledge of Good and Evil*. From this and other sources we present some examples of Munch's interpretive prose style.

Much of what Munch wrote reflects his personal experiences. We know that this is so in the case of *The Scream*; on a sketch from 1891 (fig. 29) he has written: "I was walking along the road with two friends — then the sun went down — the sky became suddenly a bloody red. I stopped, leant against the fence, unutterably tired — tongues of fire and blood lay across the blue-black fjord. My friends walked on, while I remained behind, shaking with fear — and I experienced the great, endless scream of nature." Munch's friend the Norwegian painter Christian Skredsvig recalls that during their time together in Nice, Munch was plagued by his inability to paint the memory of a sunset which had filled him with fear: "Red like blood. No, it *was* clotted blood. None but he would experience it in this way. Everyone else would think of clouds. 'He longs for the impossible, and despair is his religion,' I thought — but I advised him to go ahead and paint it. — The result was his remarkable *Scream*" (fig. 39).

The Voice (fig. 43) is related to another text which has all the signs of being based on personal experience:

Stand up on this clump of grass a moment so that I can look into your eyes —
You are taller than I — I'll stand up on the grass, then I shall be able to look into your eyes —
How pale you are in the moonlight, how dark your eyes are —

they are so large that they cover half the heavens —
I can hardly make out your features — but I glimpse your white teeth when you smile —
I feel a bit cold — how dark the wood is —
Don't you see an animal in there — is it a stone — or a head — the head of a snake —
I believe you're smiling —
When we stand like this — and my eyes look into your eyes — in the pale moonlight — then, you know — slender hands weave invisible threads — which are bound round my heart — are led from my eyes — through your large dark eyes — into your heart —
Your eyes are so big now that you're near me
They are like two big, dark heavens

Other texts are of a more generally descriptive nature, or take the form of ruminations with their origins in personal experiences, without such direct reference to specific circumstances as the foregoing. The text for *Jealousy* (fig. 61), from *The Tree of Knowledge of Good and Evil*, is one such:

A mysterious look the madman's
these two piercing eyes
are concentrated as
in a crystal many
reflections. — the look is
penetrating, interested
hateful, full of
love the essence
of she whom they
all have in common

Or a prose poem which automatically suggests *Madonna*;

A pause when all the world
stopped turning
your face contains all the beauty
of the earth
your crimson lips
like ripening fruit glide
from each other as though in pain
the smile of a corpse
now life stretches out a hand
to death
the link is forged,
the thousand generations that
are gone join the
thousand generations yet to come

Here we encounter the strange association of death with sex that was so typical of the era, an association which seems to have dominated Munch's view of eroticism for at least part of his life. The attitude probably has its roots in an emotional block which prevented him from fully experiencing the personal warmth that is part of physical closeness in a relationship. The high rate of death in childbed in those days may have had its effect on the way in which a sensitive man perceived the possible consequences of the sexual encounter between man and woman. In addition we have Munch's own view of himself as the bearer of destructive genes, something to which he refers several times in his manuscripts. He writes that "the great power of love in me was dead — the poison of tuberculosis brought grief and the fear of life into my home as a child — killed off faith in life and childhood joy, and destroyed my home"; and, elsewhere: "Sickness (hereditary tuberculosis and neurasthenia) made it impossible for me to marry". When a child, his consumptive mother had given birth in the shadow of death.

When *The Frieze of Life* was exhibited in Berlin in 1902, the pictures dealing with love were divided into two groups — *Seeds of Love* and *Flowering and Passion of Love*. Ten other paintings, grouped under the titles *Life Anxiety* and *Death*, were presented as a continuation of these. Thus the frieze was expanded to represent a view of life that connected its creative and destructive forces in a way also symbolized in the 1899 *Metabolism* (fig. 79), which has already been described. In 1918 Munch himself wrote, "The motif is perhaps not directly related to the idea expressed in the other fields, but all the same it is as necessary for the wholeness of the frieze as the buckle is for the belt." Life comes full circle in this painting, so that the presence of death at the moment of conception in *Madonna* takes on a meaning in terms of this larger perspective.

Many of the angst and death motifs in *The Frieze of Life* can be traced to Munch's personal experiences; *The Scream* (fig. 39) has already been mentioned — the painting shows the view from the hill at Ekeberg in Kristiania looking towards the sea, with the jutting point at Aker and the surrounding hills. *Evening on Karl Johan Street* (fig. 34) describes a feeling of deep depression and alienation arising from a tense erotic situation — Munch had just met his lover, who had merely smiled and continued on her way. The motifs dealing with death reflect tragic events within Munch's family circle in his own childhood — the death of his sister (*Death in the Sickroom*, fig. 56, and *By the Deathbed (Fever)*, fig. 37) and of his mother (*The Dead Mother and the Child*, fig. 75) in the presence of their loved ones — Munch himself, his two sisters, father, and aunt. All three paintings are arranged with great care. The figures seem emotionally isolated from one another and from the observer, with the exception of the little girl in *The Dead Mother and the Child* and the woman in *Death in the Sickroom*. They address us directly as observers and as participators, and by their physical attitudes and the expressions on their faces they convey the meaning of the painting.

The dead and the dying are placed off-center in all three paintings, or rendered passive, peripheral figures — the pictures are not about them, but about the presence of death itself in the room.

The paintings in *The Frieze of Life* belong to the symbolic 1890s. They are based on personal experiences, being in effect studies of the life-forces, carried out with an urgent intensity. Something Munch wrote in later life, in a short manuscript entitled *Diary of a Mad Poet*, is applicable also to his painting: "In the same way as anatomy is discussed in Leonardo's drawings, here the anatomy of the soul is discussed — the mechanics of the soul . . . my task is the study of the soul, which is to say, the study of myself — used myself as an anatomical soul-specimen." In this light, his observations on his own notes may also be understood as a description of his paintings: "a quasi-scientific project," an examination of human beings in the grip of the terrifying life-forces, published, not in the form of a thesis with footnotes, but as pictures having a documentary value: "My art is about the process of self-understanding" — "In my art I have tried to explain my life and its meaning. — I have also hoped to make life clearer for others." Such an attitude, implying as it does the need for openness and courage, points directly back to Hans Jæger and the bohemian attitude towards life — and even further back to the great confessional artists of previous ages, such as Michel de Montaigne and Jean-Jacques Rousseau.

Munch's wish to see *The Frieze of Life* brought together under one roof, and within an architectural framework specifically designed for it, was never to be realized. Major parts of the cycle were sold to the Norwegian National Gallery and other galleries. Copies painted later by Munch to fill the gaps in his own collection sometimes lack the power of the originals.

On a couple of occasions, Munch worked on decorations for rooms which gave him the opportunity to utilize some of the same ideas as those which underlie *The Frieze of Life*. We know of three such decorative projects. The first of these was the so-called *Linde Frieze*, commissioned by Dr. Max Linde of Lübeck for use in the nursery at his house. The choice of motif, however, meant that Linde could not use the frieze; it was never hung, and is today to be found in the Munch Museum (fig. 97). The frieze is interesting because it provides clear evidence of the way in which Munch was at that time trying to break away from the linear and decorative style, with Art Nouveau influences, which he had cultivated throughout the symbolist 1890s.

The next wall decoration was commissioned by Max Reinhardt for the foyer of his newly established theater in Berlin in 1906. It was later removed and today is distributed among various museums and in private ownership. Although painted a couple of years after the Linde series, the *Reinhardt Frieze* bears a much closer stylistic resemblance to the paintings in the original frieze of life. The large canvases are painted in thin but radiantly clear colors, with brushstrokes that raise them to the level of lyrical essays (fig. 109).

The third series was done in 1922 for the Freia Chocolate factory in Oslo, and still hangs in its original site in the factory canteen. These Freia paintings show a frieze of life without its darker side, a lyrical account of the unfolding of life's processes among the trees, by the edge of the sea. Another series, depicting workers in an urban setting, was never realized (fig. 152).

All three projects were conceived of from the outset as monumental in character. But there is another small series of a quite different character — the six paintings which Munch called *The Green Room*, painted in Warnemünde in the summer of 1907 (figs. 112, 113). This series has been described earlier as most clearly demonstrating a transitional phase in Munch's art as he moved away from the decorative Art Nouveau style. The six paintings are executed in an impulsive, expressionist style which is ideally suited to their theme. Reflecting, perhaps, Munch's affair with Tulla Larsen, they show scenes from a whorehouse in which the partners come together without emotional commitment, and in which the only passions present are jealous and murderous. Rather more personal are two series which seem to reflect Edvard Munch's own relationship with women, probably models. One, done in 1914-15, describes in two paintings and a sketch in oils a visit to Munch's house in Åsgårdstrand (fig. 133); the second, from 1919-20, shows interior scenes from Ekely featuring Munch and a model (figs. 147, 149). Munch depicts himself in the grip of strong feelings. In *Model by the Wicker Chair* (fig. 149) he conveys, merely through his rendering of the bedclothes, the powerful sense of emotional confusion and tension which probably lay behind these works. Arne Eggum uses the expression "reckless self-searching" to describe them, and calls them "a description of the loneliness of an aging man among people and objects."

Munch also worked on the ideas in *The Frieze of Life* in other mediums than painting. We know of fragments from a series of graphic works on *Life*, and another called *18 Scenes from the Life of a Modern Soul*. He also published three folders of graphic works. One contains eight thematically unrelated etchings, in an edition by Meier-Graefe, who was working at the time for the Bing Gallery in Paris. The

Munch's house, Skrubben, in Kragerø. He lived here from 1909 - c. 1915. Munch Museum.

second shows scenes from Dr. Linde's home and family life in Lübeck. The third was done by Munch during his hospitalization in Copenhagen in 1908-09. Based in part on sketches done years before, it was called by him *Alpha and Omega* (fig. 119). Here, with humor, irony, and some bitterness, Munch describes a love affair between two beautiful young people on a deserted island at the dawn of time. The woman's erotic curiosity eventually brings her into contact with all the beasts on the island in a fashion which has tragic consequences for herself and for the poor man.

The war of 1914-18 affected Munch deeply, even though he was able to observe it from the comfort of the sidelines. Seven lithographs entitled *Ragnarok IV* (fig. 142) testify to his involvement. It is interesting to note the way in which he returns to the theme of the transformation of matter treated in *The Frieze of Life*, and in three lithographs from 1915-16 views the tragic events on the battlefield of Europe from the perspective of eternity (fig. 146).

Some of these themes continued to interest Munch: towards the end of the 1920s he was still working on a composition in which a preliminary version of *The Human Mountain*, produced in connection with the murals at Oslo University, was placed in the center, flanked by *Ragnarok* and *The Rainbow* (fig. 150).

Munch's last larger decorative project was for the walls of the proposed City Hall in Oslo. He produced a number of sketches (fig. 157) and large-scale outlines involving themes from working life, but the project came to nothing — by the beginning of the 1930s he was no longer physically strong enough for such rigorous and time-consuming work.

Munch's most impressive frieze was finally completed after years of hard work, however. This was the monumental oil paintings on the walls of the assembly hall of Oslo

University, with which Munch was intensely preoccupied from 1909 to 1916 (figs. 128 to 131).

It was typical of Munch's vitality that, as soon as he heard of the closed competition arranged to celebrate the University's centenary, he entered and set to work on his designs at once, although he had only just emerged from an eight-months' stay a in hospital. The full story of this competition is lengthy and complicated, and cannot be gone into in any detail here. To begin with, when the sketches were presented in March 1910, Munch showed two ideas which were later developed — one in which an old man is telling a story to a little boy (fig. 131), and the other showing an enormous mountain of climbing human beings reaching out towards a great, shining sun. The first theme was worked on and eventually mounted on one of the long walls in the hall, but of *The Human Mountain* (fig. 150) only *The Sun* has survived. It became the dominant motif of the hall, painted as Edvard Munch saw it from his house Skrubben in Kragerø, rising in the east, its bright morning rays shining over the sea approaches to the city (fig. 128).

This new painting of the sun was presented when the results of the competition's second round were shown in July 1911. In addition to *The Sun* and *History*, Munch had completed nine other full-scale designs. The dimensions were large — the panels for the long walls measured $14\frac{3}{4} \times 38\frac{1}{6}$ feet, *The Sun* $14\frac{3}{4} \times 25\frac{1}{2}$ feet. He worked unceasingly on this project throughout the next five years, until the sections were put in position in 1916. They were also exhibited abroad on several occasions. The whole series was shown in quarter-size at the Berlin Secession in 1913, where it attracted widespread attention. A suggestion that the whole work be acquired for the University of Jena perhaps provided the impetus needed to persuade the Oslo authorities finally to make up their minds to accept Munch's designs and commission him to finish them for the hall.

The symbolism in these huge and colorful motifs is, on the surface at least, relatively straightforward. A white-hot sun, explosively glowing, rises over the horizon, casting life-giving energy all around. Humans who have been lying asleep rise up from the rocks and stretch in the sunlight (fig. 129). On the upper side-sections the naked figures stand in a glory of light and ecstatic color and reach out with their arms towards the flood of light.

On both the long side walls Munch has painted figures from Norwegian daily life, placing them in situations which give them an elevated, symbolic significance. Beneath the great oak — symbol of life itself — "in a remote landscape imbued with the sense of history sits an aged man from the fjords" who has, in Munch's own words, "struggled and fought his way through life. Now he sits with his fund of memories and tells stories to a spellbound little boy."

The whole landscape is, in a sense, an elevated presentation of the rocky seascape off Kragerø, where Munch painted the picture. The symbolism is clear: through these everyday people Munch presents a picture of the way in which knowledge is handed down from generation to generation in a process which is at the heart of an institute of learning such as the University.

On the opposite wall is the *Alma Mater* (fig. 130) in the form of a mother suckling a baby, with children playing around her. The landscape here is from the other side of the Oslo fjord, where Munch owned an estate at Ramme, near Hvitsten. The landscape in *History* is heroic, hard and barren; in *Alma Mater* it is gentle and fertile. The white birch trunks contrast with the hard oak in *History*, and in the trunk of the pine tree we see the suggestion of a child's face, recalling the fetus which was once painted in the treetrunk in that picture which Munch called the buckle in the belt that was *The Frieze of Life - Metabolism* (fig. 79). Munch points out the connection himself in his program note for the exhibition of *The Frieze of Life* in 1918: "The frieze of life and the university decorations are united in the frieze's painting of Man and Woman among the trees, with the golden city in the background."

Four smaller canvases are shown in pairs on either side of the two main motifs: next to *History* is a symbolic representation of chemistry. A young couple are bent in wonder over a chemist's flask in which a chemical reaction is taking place, giving off fumes which drift up towards the heavens, where new life is created. *New Beams* symbolizes physics — a young couple surrounded by glowing particles of energy which radiate from their heads and pass through their surroundings in waves. They are "half conscious, illuminated by new beams, heart to heart," in Munch's own words. *Alma Mater* is flanked by symbols of fertility, inspiration, and life-energy — young women pick apples while a young couple drink from the life-giving waters that cascade down the mountainside. A university's obligation to educate, and the sphere of its activity, have habitually been seen in terms of traditional allegories: St. George killing the dragon of ignorance, a blindfolded Justice with sword and scales. Munch was a creator of images on a different level, preferring to take his symbols from the world of everyday life about him, invest them with a new significance and thereby rejuvenate the known and the familiar.

As we have seen, Munch himself stressed the connection between *The Frieze of Life* and *The Aula Decorations*: "The frieze of life depicts in close-up the sorrows and joys of individual life, while the Aula decorations depict the great and eternal forces of life in the widest sense."

Individual thematic groupings: Landscapes, workers, portraits, and self-portraits

A separate book could be written on the subject of Munch as a landscape painter. Throughout his life, and in a wide variety of ways, he painted the landscape — let us look at some of the most important phases of his work in this area.

From Munch's earliest years as an open-air painter, we have woodland studies and paintings of lakes done in the regions around Kristiania where he grew up (fig. 5). Arne Eggum draws particular attention to an unusual group of studies from the Nordmarka in tones of gold and grey "which make one think of the French painter Camille Corot." Only rarely, even in these sketches, do we find pure landscapes. There is always one or more houses to indicate the effect of human beings on nature, and this is also the case with the large open-air paintings in impressionist style which Munch executed during his summer stays on the Oslo fjord towards the late 1880s. Yet what we do notice in these is the way in which the atmospheric content of the paintings is reinforced: the time of day is often evening, and a lyrical melancholy in the landscape echoes the mood of some clearly depicted foreground figure, as in *Evening* (fig. 13) and *Eventide*, both from the summer of 1888 in Vrengen. These are closely related in spirit to the magnificent *Inger on the Beach* (fig. 17), done the following year in Åsgårdstrand, in which a landscape tending towards the abstract conveys atmosphere in a quite new way. Through her coloring and her attitude, the sister's sitting figure achieves an emotional harmony with the landscape, thus showing us landscape as the mirror of the soul.

Inger on the Beach points ahead to paintings forming part of *The Frieze of Life*, where abstract landscapes and figures in psychologically fraught states were brought into meaningful relationships with one another, and in which the landscape, through the play of line and color, comments upon the mood-states of the human subjects depicted. All northern dwellers recognize the mystery and magic in Munch's paintings of the light summer nights.

On certain rare occasions, Munch empties his landscapes of people and allows the mood itself to become predominant, as in *The Mystery of a Summer Night* (fig. 32). This was Munch's first step in the direction of a purely symbolic depiction of landscape, involving the expressive treatment of compositional elements and color to evoke an enigmatic and magical content. To enhance the feeling of the supernatural, Munch has turned one of the stones on the beach into a ghostly head, which further heightens the painting's similarity to his own description of wandering on a summer's night along the beach:

It was evening — I walked by the sea —
there was moonlight between the clouds
the stones against the background of water
mysterious, like sea-dwellers,
with their great white heads ... and laughing —
some on the beach, others underwater ...
I heard the sighing and swishing of water
round the rocks — long grey clouds along the horizon —
everything seems dead — a landscape of death from another world

Munch developed the theme of the symbolic landscape in a series of winter and summer studies of unusual power painted in 1900 and 1901 at Ljan, east of Oslo, looking out over the fjord (figs. 83, 84). Few of these include people; they derive effect instead from the use of color and the suggestive treatment of the landscape. Here and there Munch suggests an unnamed presence in the form of trees which resemble people, and bright points of light which seem like eyes. These strengthen the sense of life in the paintings without disturbing the character of the landscape.

From about 1900 on, the landscapes continue this move away from the introverted world of the 1890s: the emotional tension is still present, but in the landscapes the atmosphere is less oppressive. *Rain* (fig. 90) from 1902 and *From Thüringerwald* (fig. 104) from around 1905 are both without obtrusive emotional overtones. After Munch settled at Kragerø, his open-air paintings of landscapes are also characterized by a greater use of daylight colors, and a monumentality which reminds us of the University murals. These trends are especially evident in his marvelous winter landscapes from Kragerø (fig. 132) and the large paintings of woodland interiors (fig. 126). Yet these works are not entirely devoid of symbolic content: the old woodcutter by a felled tree, done in 1913 (fig. 137), may be simply a scene from the life of a local worker; it may also be Munch's comment on the transitory nature of life.

In the years that followed, Munch produced a great many landscapes. These describe the different surroundings he found himself in as he moved from place to place — from Kragerø to Hvitsten, to Jeløya, and finally to Ekely in 1916. Perhaps the most beautiful canvases of the later period of Munch's life are those he painted at Ekely in the 1920s, in which a red barn forms the centerpiece of his depictions of late winter and early spring. These are painted with the fluency of a watercolorist, using colors thinned with turpentine to achieve a remarkably lyrical power (fig. 156, 163).

One group of paintings, all featuring working people, has been the subject of a special study by Gerd Woll. In Munch's early years, such paintings were probably not the result of any specific or unusual interest in the subject of workers; as a naturalist painter, he simply painted them as part of the surrounding world, in much the same spirit as many of his contemporaries did.

But certain works done after the turn of the century, mostly in Germany, reveal a deeper interest. *The Fisherman* (fig. 85) and *The Fisherman and His Daughter* (fig. 86) both from 1902, reveal a quite different degree of psychological interest in their subjects. Munch sees them as individuals at the same time as he sees them as typical of their class. We sense a growing concern for the living conditions of his models: *Worker and Child* (fig. 116) from 1908 shows a line of dark and apparently joyless male figures, broken when one of them leaves the group to embrace the bright figure of a child with outstretched arms, as yet untouched by the harsh conditions of adult life.

When Munch settled in Kragerø after his return to Norway in 1909, working people became a part of his daily life in quite a different way. Some, like the old seaman Børre Eriksen, fascinated him more than others; he immortalized Eriksen by using him to personify the idea and value of tradition in his University painting *History* (fig. 131).

We know that Munch admired the courage with which ordinary people faced the adversities of everyday life. In this he was also probably emotionally attracted to a "romance of the soil" which was current at the time, a feeling which found its literary expression in Knut Hamsun's novel *Growth of the Soil*. Among the earliest sketches for the University paintings we find a sower and a plowman, and from the lush Østfold district, and later still from Ekely, we meet foresters, haymakers, plowmen and other harvest workers (fig. 144). The most impressive is the large *Man in the Cabbage Field*, from 1916, in which the figure is gathering the earth's abundant harvest of riches.

On a journey home from Bergen to Kragerø in 1909, Munch met some of the new industrial proletariat, gangs who were working on some of the many large projects under way in Norway at that time. He at once developed his sketchbook drawings into larger compositions which by stages became the monumental *Workers in the Snow* of 1913 (fig. 135): out of a desolate mountain landscape, three foreground figures advance upon us. As always, Munch's depiction of character is striking — but here the group has a nobility which suggests that Munch also wanted to communicate the strength of working people and the dignity of work itself.

As depiction of the proletariat, *Workers in the Snow* can be compared with the almost contemporary *Workers on Their Way Home* (fig. 136) painted in Moss between 1913-15. In the wake of the 1917 Russian revolution critics commonly interpreted it as symbolizing the victorious advance of the working class, but in fact this view of the work is more difficult to sustain than it is with *Workers in the Snow*, where the men with their spades are rendered with a self-assured monumentality and something of the same power as the group in *Bathing Men* (fig. 115). The main figures in *Workers on Their Way Home* are not depicted heroically. They have large, hollow eyes, and move forward through a swaying perspective which recalls the disturbing paintings of the 1890s, in particular *Evening on Karl Johan Street* (fig. 34). There are other interesting aspects of *Workers on Their Way Home*: Munch had clearly been preoccupied with the problem of movement, and by doubling the outlines of the figure to the right and working on the position of the legs of the workers on the left, he tried to convey an impression of strong forward motion.

According to Gerd Woll, Munch wanted to collect several motifs of this type under a general heading of *The Frieze of the Worker*, but never completed the project. The idea of a frieze was suggested for the Freia Chocolate factory in Oslo in 1921, but here an idyll is presented in richly colored scenes, showing workers leaving the factory, walking in the town, together with their families — workers who live in pleasant houses behind white fences and go for long walks in the beautiful countryside surrounding the city (fig. 152).

Throughout the 1920s, workers continued to occupy an important part of Munch's thematic world, not least because he hoped to be given the commission to decorate the walls of the planned City Hall in Oslo. In large, dramatic sketches he depicted the work of clearing the site and the erection of the huge building (fig. 157), and he produced monumental elaborations on his *Workers in the Snow* painting as suggestions for wall decorations. The last of these — which were never used — stem from the period 1929-1933, when he had a new winter studio built for himself at Ekely, which gave him the opportunity to study building workers at close quarters (fig. 159).

This whole cycle of motifs featuring fishermen, farm workers, and building and factory workers as its chief actors raises the question of Munch's own political and social orientation. This probably changed somewhat over the years. As the child of a relatively impoverished intellectual family he later in life clearly felt that contempt for the comfortable, moneyed middle class which is not uncommon under such circumstances. During important periods of his life he moved in radical circles; his friend Hans Jæger was a notorious anarchist and a central figure in the bohemians' war against the accepted norms and values of bourgeois society of the 1880s. Munch's own attitude was not doctrinaire; he took a deep interest in world developments and was deeply stirred by the historic importance of the Russian revolution. During the 1920s he read Marx, and numerous quotes attest to the fact that he was sympathetic towards the progress of socialism. Yet his circle of acquaintances was wide and included members of the bourgeoisie as well as aristocrats and radicals. In fact, he never joined any movement, and never expressed his views in public; he knew quite well that his own struggle took place in the world of art.

In some 400 painted portraits and using other graphic media, Munch emerges as a revitalizing force for this particular art form in his own time. As ever, he worked on themes and material from the world immediately surrounding him, which in his first years as a painter meant his family and his friends. His first full-scale work is the portrait of his friend Karl Jensen-Hjell (fig. 12), painted after Munch's first short stay in Paris in 1885. It combines elements from the European tradition of portrait painting with a personal cheekiness which on its first showing to the public did not fail to create controversy. Other portraits of his Kristiania friends followed. In 1889 — clearly influenced by Christian Krohg — he painted Hans Jæger (fig. 16) as a burnt-out and disillusioned man in a friend's humble apartment in Oslo. A contrast with the Jæger portrait is provided by the firm and stylistically extremely interesting portrait of Jacob Bratland (fig. 30) done in 1891-92, in which the modernist décor of the background recalls the Art Déco of the 1920s. There are portraits of friends from the Berlin days, like that of August Strindberg (fig. 31) from 1892, in an impressionist style that recalls the paintings he did in Nice. The writer was not particularly happy with the portrait, and four years later in Paris Munch made another and more impressive attempt in the form of a black-and-white lithograph. Another friend from Berlin was the Polish writer Stanislaw Przybyszewski (fig. 63), whom Munch portrayed in several versions, including one in which his detached, sensitive face is seen over crossbones. His wife Dagny Juel (fig. 36) is painted full-length; she is erotic and inviting against a gleaming blue background, with faint concentric circles around her head, as though Munch were trying to convey the radiance of her personality in the shape of a magnetic field.

The large full-length portraits painted after the turn of the century are in a class of their own: Munch's Norwegian friend Consul Sandberg from 1901 (fig. 120), a delightful celebration of this exuberant, life-loving man; a painter friend, Ludvig Karsten (fig. 99), done in 1905, and the brilliantly gifted but obviously arrogant Walter Rathenau (fig. 111).

Later still, on his return to Norway in 1909, came a series of full-length portraits of friends. The first of these was Munch's doctor Daniel Jacobson (fig. 121), painted while Munch was still a patient in Copenhagen; the portrait of the dominating physician is not without malice. Munch described the circumstances surrounding the creation of the painting to Rolf Stenersen: Jacobson "was like the pope there among all those white-clad nurses and us sickly patients . . . but I felt I wanted to have my say in the matter too, and I got him to pose for me. I put him there, powerful, legs apart, in front of the bright fires of hell. He pleaded for mercy then . . . tame as a dove. Pope Jacobson became my prisoner." When Munch painted, it was he who was master of the situation, he who dominated his surroundings.

The portraits of Munch's Norwegian friends which he did after his return to Kragerø in 1909 are not characterized by the same degree of conflict and tension. They show a small circle of close friends and acquaintances whom Munch had known for years, and he portrays them insightfully, in a spirit of friendly tolerance. There is Christian Gierløff (fig. 124), large and jovial, greeting the observer; and Munch's childhood friend Thorvald Stang (fig. 122), a slightly down-

at-heel figure — Stang was another, like Munch, who had had his share of troubles with John Barleycorn. The cheekiest portrait is that of Jens Thiis (fig. 123), director of the National Gallery. Thiis is said to have been unsettled by the painting and to have fled the sittings for it. Although signed, it seemingly remained unfinished, but renders that posturing side to Thiis' character which was well known to his contemporaries.

Munch's ability to capture and express character is also apparent in his portraits of children: the four little girls from Åsgårdstrand (figs. 101) and Dr. Linde's four sons (fig. 96) are all distinct from one another, in terms of both age and personality. The powerfully decorative approach in these paintings is reinforced in many of Munch's graphic works — a wide-ranging group of portraits that includes some of his finest depictions of women, such as the imperiously beautiful Eva Mudocci (fig. 92) and the delicate etching The Nurse (fig. 117), done at Dr. Jacobson's clinic in Copenhagen.

The portraits comprise a rich and varied grouping within Munch's art and stretch over a long period of time. It is difficult to venture any general characterization, but they do have in common a depth of character analysis and revealing quality not always flattering to the subject. Munch looks for those states of mind which leave their mark on a person: he tries to capture the expression of character in the look of an eye and knows how to use the expressive power of hands. The accessories he uses are few and understated — a bookcase in the background for the museum director Harry Graf Kessler (fig. 98); a barely visible box of matches in the hands of Fritz Frölich (fig. 158), a manufacturer of matchsticks. Clothes are significant, both as an indicator of a model's social class and as expressions of personality: consider Hans Jæger (fig. 16), buttoned-up and freezingly shabby, his battered felt hat worn even indoors in the cold room; Max Linde's neat, tidy bourgeois children (fig. 96); the touch of bohemianism about the rich Christen Sandberg (fig. 120); and the correct and icily elegant Walter Rathenau (fig. 111), magnate of modern industry, writer, and future minister of foreign affairs.

The lack of accessories means that Munch's rendering of his subject's personality depends heavily on his posing of the model — the body language, to use the modern term — the play of color, and the relationship between the figure and surrounding space. Here Munch shows the true extent of his expressive powers. Dagny Juel (fig. 36) melts into the soft, dreamy blue surroundings; Munch's own white face stares out at us from the black surface as if from a gravestone, in his 1895 lithograph. Daniel Jacobson (fig. 121), powerful, dominating, a manipulator of human passions and minds, stands like a magician, his dark shadow blue-black against the burning yellow and shrieking red. More often than not the figures fill the surfaces, the model standing well to the fore in the picture, legs often painted as though they were about to take the one step that would enable their owner to come out from the canvas and join us. The confrontation with the observer is direct, the frontal pose dominating.

Yet in spite of this apparent physical nearness in which they are "just a step away," Munch's models have an air of permanence about them. They "strike a pose," as we say, and through these poses manage to convey something fundamental to their nature, as interpreted by Munch. This is emphasized by what we know of Munch's use of photographs as optical aids in order to fix a pose or an expression, and by the stories of how irritated he would become when one of his subjects changed clothes or hairstyle while work on the painting was in process.

Numerous anecdotes have circulated concerning Munch the portrait painter, and many exhibit such a high degree of internal consistency that they would seem to be accurate and trustworthy. It was evidently important for Munch to try to build up a personal relationship with his model, something which might be achieved through close contact over a long stretch of time. The Esche family, for example, children and parents, were painted over the course of a few days after Munch had been living in their home for some weeks. The painting of the Perls was done at Jeløya, near Moss, where the models had been staying for a month. Sometimes Munch would approach directly the people he wished to paint, as was the case with the director of the Bank of Norway, Oluf Rygg. At other times, portraiture was his way out of financial trouble — the 3,000 German marks he received from the Esche family in Weimar was a great deal of money in 1905, as were the 5,000 Norwegian kroner he received for his portrait of Prime Minister Otto Blehr in the early 1930s. His friend Albert Kollmann worked hard to secure new commissions for Munch, but his overwrought and nervous mental condition meant that he was not always able to accept them. Nevertheless, he continued to paint portraits throughout the 1920s and 1930s, his last being that of Erik Pedersen, director of the Freia Chocolate Company. Pedersen wrote a description of the whole process and indicated that the portrait was signed on October 23, 1943, just three months before the artist's death.

I have already advanced a claim for Munch as one of the great painters of self-portraits in the history of art. When Johan Langaard and Reidar Revold published his self-portraits in 1947, their total came to more than eighty. The actual figure is even higher, especially if we include all these times that Munch painted himself as a participant in his pictures.

The self-portraits from his youth are few and small in scale. The first, from 1881-2 (fig. 6), bears traces of the classically oriented instruction he was receiving at the Drawing School at that time: a conventional modelling of form in terms of light and shade expresses a concept marked by a certain pre-Raphaelite sensuality, and more than a touch of arrogance. The sensitive mouth and the skeptical, slightly remote look appear again in the 1886 portrait (fig. 15), but here the technique has undergone a dramatic change — the surface is scratched and scraped, and in several places the canvas is left bare. But then, it was painted in the same year as *The Sick Child* (fig. 11).

The 1890s were the years of Munch's symbolic portraits, like the large blue one with a cigarette from 1895 (fig. 58), probably inspired by one of August Strindberg's photographic self-portraits for which the writer used a similar dramatic lighting. Against an imprecise background, Munch's figure emerges from the drifting cigarette smoke almost like a spiritualist medium, staring at us with the direct, penetrating gaze of a seer. Behind him the darkness thickens in those pregnant shadows which Munch used so often during this period. The painting is related to the lithographic self-portrait from the same year (fig. 59), in which the face is viewed from the front, staring directly ahead but this time with the veiled look familiar to us from many of the descriptions of Munch. The face is seen against a completely black background, with no other distracting elements save a skeleton arm, *memento mori*. With the name "Edvard Munch" written out, and the year 1895, the whole composition seems almost like a sketch for a gravestone. Additionally, the self-portrait represents one of Munch's earliest attempts at a lithograph, and his immediate mastery of the new technique is impressive. The use of the lithographic pen is supplemented by fine scorings across the surface of the stone, creating a remarkably sophisticated print.

Three portraits from the period after 1900 are of particular interest. In the self-confident study with paintbrushes from 1904 (fig. 100), Munch depicts himself as an elegant man conventionally attired in necktie and starched collar. The brushes have been dipped in the red that he so often used in his depictions of emotionally loaded themes. The room around him is clearly defined, his pose is self-assured. In *Self-portrait in Weimar* (fig. 106), from 1906, the atmosphere is quite different. The facial expression and slumped posture are eloquent of deep depression. Again, there is the use of a swaying perspective between the surfaces of the tables which seems to make the room contract, increasing the psychological tension in the painting. The *Self-portrait at Professor Jacobson's Hospital* (fig. 118) from 1909 shows us the convalescent — a dark figure set against a yellow background, with the sunlight flowing through the window. The position of the body and the expression on the face both exude a somewhat humorless air of determination.

At times it is difficult to distinguish between genuine self-portraits and those renderings in which Munch takes a place as one of the actors in the scene. There is an obvious self-deprecation, for example, in the way in which Munch depicted himself as the aging Peer Gynt dancing with Anitra in his illustrations for Ibsen's play (fig. 139). The drawing was done in 1913, when Munch had just turned 50, and clearly represents the aging painter's attitude towards his own sexuality. Similarly, *Man and Woman* (fig. 103) from 1905 is clearly Munch's statement of the isolation and distance he had felt in his relationship with Tulla Larsen, which had been dramatically broken off three years earlier. The male figure in *The Flower of Pain* (fig. 71) seems to be modeled on Munch, and the whole scene is in accord with a view he expressed several times in his notebooks, that art has to be nourished by the artist's own blood. The statement is familiar to us from Hans Jæger's speech given in self-defence at the Supreme Court in 1886, but he — and Munch too, for that matter — may well have been quoting from Nietzsche's *Also Sprach Zarathustra*. The section on reading and writing begins thus: "Of all that has been written, I love only that which someone writes with his own blood. Write with blood: and you will see that blood is spirit." ("Von allem Geschriebenen liebe ich nur Das, was Einer mit seinem Blute schreibt. Schreibe mit Blut: und du wirst erfahren, dass Blut Geist ist.")

Munch's long life as a self-observer was to conclude with a small series of exceptional portraits of himself as an old man. None of these can be dated precisely, although *Self-portrait between the Clock and the Bed* (fig. 164) is perhaps one of the very last. Munch stands attentive, upright, and looking more worn out than he does even in the last photographs. It is hard to know how far one may go in interpreting this painting, but it is tempting to see a meaning in the contrast between the lit room, with its friendly yellow walls, and the darkness in the unknown room beyond the open door in the background. That the clock face is shown without hands may be simply a matter of chance — Munch was never fussy about details. All the same, it is interesting to recall in this context an expression commonly used among the Swedes to comment upon a death — "He has gone out of time" — that is to say, into eternity. Take away the clock's hands, and its value as a measurer of time is gone too. And one last thing: in front of Munch's feet we see a reflection rather like that thrown by the lattice of a window, a cross-shape which is used with clear symbolic intent in some of the older drawings.

Munch's house, Ekely, on the outskirts of Oslo, where he lived from 1916 until his death in January 1944. Munch Museum.

Munch as a graphic artist

Thus far we have considered Munch's art in its entirety, without distinguishing particularly between the different techniques he used. All the same, a short section devoted exclusively to his work as a graphic artist is necessary — he was, after all, one of the greatest masters of the graphic arts, and his graphic work represents a most significant part of his œuvre.

As in everything else, Munch was a great experimenter as a graphic artist and used all manner of unconventional techniques when he set to work on metal plate, lithographic stone, or woodblock for printing. He scratched the sandstone, worked to find his own way of achieving subtle effects in his etchings, sawed up his woodblocks like jigsaw puzzles, colored the various pieces individually, and printed the whole thing in one go. Munch was certainly not the first to utilize such techniques, but he developed their capacity to produce supremely elegant results.

The technical variety which characterizes the prints is just one expression of the wealth of energy which made his work as a graphic artist a continual process, in the course of which complete works were created but a final goal was never reached. A theme would be tried out and developed, different techniques were used, the motifs varied by addition or subtraction. The same motif might change character completely, from a richly detailed engraved plate to monumental simplicity in a woodcut — the best example of this being *The*

Kiss (figs. 55, 72, 73). Even where the medium did not change, Munch was capable of achieving an astonishing variety of improvizations on the same theme by changing the colors from one print to the next: indeed, the Munch Museum possesses long series of many of the most important works, in which no two prints are alike coloristically. This method of working also served to radically alter the nature of a motif, revealing it in new aesthetic and psychological perspectives.

Munch was already a mature artist when he took up graphic arts, and he took them up at a time when they were being talked about again not simply as a means of illustrating publications but as an art-form in their own right. There were many reasons for this — the historical importance of men like Rembrandt and Goya, the contemporary influences of the new poster art and of Japanese woodcuts, and the efforts of individual artists like the German Max Klinger, the Swiss Félix Vallotton, the Belgian Felicien Rops, and the French artists Henri Toulouse-Lautrec, Emil Bernard, and Paul Gauguin, whose woodcuts must have particularly impressed Munch.

In November 1894, Munch wrote home to his family with the news that he was now etching in copper. This continued in 1895 in Berlin, where he also took up lithography. In 1896, having moved to Paris, he began working with woodcuts there. Through public and private collections, and magazines and books, Munch had access to a rich source of inspirational material, and a number of first-class printers were available: Gustav Schiefler (who was the first to publish Munch's graphic work) mentions Sabo, Angerer, Felsing, Liebmann, and Lasally in Berlin, as well as Clot and Lemercier in Paris. There were still others in Copenhagen, and in Norway. Munch also printed his own work, and in 1913, after finally settling in Norway, he acquired his own printing press. This was operated partly by outside printers and partly by Munch himself. Munch took an active part in the printing of his various motifs, so that the final results accurately represent his artistic intentions to an unusual degree.

Munch produced a quite exceptional number of graphic works; the index records over 800 different motifs. He did not keep a close record of how many copies of each work were printed, but we know that they were distributed widely. The prints found at Ekely after his death were brought to the Munch Museum, where a core of some 6,000 - 7,000 prints represents the most interesting works out of a collection more than twice as large. In addition, the Museum possesses a large collection of lithographic stones, metal plates used for etchings, and woodblocks for woodcuts; the latter in particular are works of art in their own right, and were exhibited at several exhibitions by Munch himself.

The motifs in much of the graphic work come from the paintings; this is particularly true of the earlier works. We find reproductions using the techniques of graphic art of several of the most important parts of *The Frieze of Life* — *The Sick Child* (figs. 49, 67), *Jealousy I* (fig. 62), *Death in the Sickroom* (fig. 57), *The Scream* (fig. 60), *Anxiety* (fig. 66), and many others. The graphic versions soon develop into independent studies which express something new about the motifs. The same joy — or the same urge to examine every side of a motif that we find in Munch as draftsman, painter, and writer is apparent here also.

Later Munch singled out specific themes for graphic treatment, themes which were not explored further in his paintings. The graphic portraits form one such independent group; another is the collection of cruel caricatures he created for his satirical drama *Free Love*. During his stay in a hospital in Copenhagen in 1909 he produced the series of lithographs called *Alpha and Omega* (fig. 119), which seemed to him at the time his most successful work; and shortly afterwards, around 1913, a small collection of unusually fine erotic etchings, clearly based on personal experience (fig. 138). Throughout his life, with different techniques assuming prominence at different times, Munch continued to produce graphic art. His last print was a new version of the portrait of his old friend Hans Jæger, King of the Bohemians, which Munch produced in the autumn of 1943 — the last year of his life (fig. 162).

Munch's faith

Throughout most of mankind's history, the meaning of works of art has been based on prevailing religious and political beliefs. The artist was by and large an interpreter of accepted truths and was quite happy to be so. Not until the first years of the century in which Munch was born — the Age of Romanticism — did the artist become the most important actor on the stage. As skepticism about the sanctity of time-honored truths spread, so did the personal vision of the intuitively gifted artist acquire an increased value. Seen from this point of view, it is clear that the symbolist artists of the 1890s saw themselves as the direct heirs of their Romantic predecessors.

Munch's view of himself as an explorer of inner realities reflects the Romantic view. The personal nature of his interpretation of life is so obvious that understanding his individual philosophy of life and individual faith becomes increasingly crucial to gaining a real understanding of his work. Let us therefore, by way of conclusion, try to say something about Munch's beliefs.

From private letters and other sources, we know that orthodox Protestantism formed the basic religious attitudes in Munch's childhood home. The children and their parents were convinced of the reality of sin and punishment at the same time as they hoped for salvation and cultivated a quite literal belief that they would all meet again beyond the grave. Such faith provided comfort and strength in difficult times, and a loving family life — within the obvious limits of bourgeois moral norms, and subject to the rigors of fatherly chastisement and admonition — was fundamental to the cultural system of which the Munch family were part. For Munch as well as his brothers and sisters, Christianity was the cornerstone of childhood faith.

Young Edvard's faith collapsed at some point during the 1880s, after he came in contact with the radical circles of the Kristiania bohemians. Hans Jæger in particular must have played a decisive role in this. The break must have been profoundly disturbing to Munch, especially as regarded his relationship with his father.

After the death of Christian Munch's wife, his religious feelings could at times assume fanatical proportions. His son soon drifted away, becoming intensely involved in a love affair with a married woman. Although Munch as an adult could no longer call himself a Christian, he retained throughout his life a need to reflect on existential mysteries at the deepest level. The words of his friend Jens Thiis, penned in 1909 and reproduced in his book published in 1933 on the occasion of Munch's seventieth birthday, apply to the artist at every stage of his life: "All the same, I am convinced that Munch's artistic temperament has a profound leaning towards the metaphysical, something which gives to his art an air of almost religious celebration of the wonders of life."

The spiritualism which flourished in Europe and the U.S. during the latter part of the nineteenth century provided a meeting ground for Christians and agnostics — a point where both could join in the exploration of an unknown reality. The Munch family's contacts with leading members of the spiritualist movement in Kristiania have recently been documented by Arne Eggum in his book *Munch and Photography*. Such contacts were probably the source of the young Munch's interest in the irrational and the supernatural — there was, after all, no contradiction in being both radical and interested in the type of supernatural phenomena which preoccupied the spiritualists. His first direct expression of interest in the great mysteries of life occurs in the autobiographical notes made during his stay at St. Cloud in winter of 1889-90.

News of his father's death reached him late in autumn of 1889, and probably helped to precipitate a period of depression during which he thought much about loved ones who were dead — his father, his sister and mother — and about death itself, the meaning of life, and the connections between it all. It was problems such as these that he discussed with the Danish writer Emanuel Goldstein, probably his closest friend at that time. He wrote the famous artistic "manifesto" already referred to, in which he prophesied an art that would explore the life-forces at their deepest level and began expressing thoughts which indicated that he was now looking to replace the rigid world-view of his religious upbringing with a more personal pantheism, based on ideas and concepts familiar to contemporary popularized natural science. Reinhold Heller stresses the influence of the German botanist and philosopher Ernst Heckel, prominent among popularizers of Darwin's theories and a man whose work was widely known and discussed by his contemporaries. Taking as his point of departure Darwin's theory of evolution, Heckel developed his own "Transmutation theory," which came to exert a direct influence on Munch's art, primarily in connection with the theme of rebirth which we have touched upon in our descriptions of Munch's use of trees in his paintings and of the 1899 painting *Metabolism* (fig. 79).

In an important note written in St. Cloud in spring of 1890, Munch's ideas about rebirth are tinged with pantheism. He tries to describe the exact occasion when the great cycle of birth and death in nature was suddenly revealed to him:

It had been cold for such a long time, and then suddenly the weather turned mild and spring-like — I went walking in the hills, enjoying the soft air and the sun — the sun was warm, only now and then a chill breath of wind — like something from a vault, mist was rising from the damp earth, there was a smell of rotting leaves — how quiet it all was — and yet I sensed the ripening life all around me — in this steaming earth with its rotting leaves — in these bare twigs — soon they would be in bud, live again — and the sun shine on the green leaves and the flowers, and the wind blow them in the sultry summer. I experienced a kind of rapture at the thought of transcience — to become one with this earth which was always in fermentation, always in the light of the sun, and which was living, living — and from my rotting body plants and trees would grow — and plants and flowers, and the sun warm them, and I inside it all, nothing would come to an end, this is eternity —

In Heller's words, "Popularized concepts of physics and evolutionary biology formed the foundations for his Decadent faith."

Notes and writings from different periods of Munch's life indicate that such problems continued to preoccupy him. All of them reinforce our picture of an agnostic who under a variety of influences never ceased to grapple with the greatest mysteries of life — the dynamics of life, the transitory nature of human existence, the relationship between man and some kind of higher power in the universe. A rather disjointed note, written in Nice on January 8 1892, illustrates this:

The seat of that power, the origin and source of that power which all living things share, which enables you to grow, to develop, to shape yourself — no-one knows that — The seeds of life — or the spirit, or soul, if you prefer — it is stupid to deny the existence of the soul — One cannot, after all, deny the existence of the seeds of life
One must believe in immortality — insofar as it can be postulated that the seeds of life, or the soul of life, continue their existence after the body is dead — This power to keep a body together — to cause growth in matter — the spirit of life — what happens to that —
Nothing vanishes — no example of this exists in Nature —

Bodies that die — do not disappear — the components of matter split up — get used in another way —
But the spirit of life, what happens to that —
No one can say — to maintain that it does not exist after the death of the body is just as stupid as trying to define it in some rigid category — or to say *where* it will exist, this spirit — To say anything at all definite about what happens after we die is stupid...
There will always be mysteries — the more things are discovered — the more there will be of inexplicable things...

Munch's continuing interest in such questions is further documented in the notebooks. In 1929 he writes: "Through it all you might say I have been a doubter, but one who has never denied or mocked religion — my doubt was more an attack on the overpietism that dominated my upbringing." He tried to summarize his faith in another note, dated June 8 1934: "My declaration of faith: I bow down before something which, if you want, one might call God — the teaching of Christ seems to me the finest there is, and Christ himself is very close to godlike — if one can use that expression."

I do not know enough about the influences that came to bear on Munch at different periods of his life, and it is difficult to distinguish those aspects of his art which reflect conscious intellectual attitudes from those which merely express ideas and views which were the common property of the age in which he lived. We can, however, trace the influences of specific works of literature and philosophy, although we cannot always be precise about the onset or duration of such influences. Munch said, for example, that he did not come across Søren Kierkegaard's *Angst* until the 1920s, at which time he was struck by the parallels between the book and his own work of the 1890s.

Other influences can be pointed to with some degree of certainty. It is clear, for example, that after the scandalous success of his exhibition in Berlin in 1892, when Munch became overnight a leading figure in radical artistic circles, he once more took part in discussions of supernatural phenomena. He read books about spiritualism and the occult and formed close friendships with the Polish writer Stanislaw Przybyszewski and with August Strindberg. Everything we know about their approaches to life indicates that Munch would have discussed with them such subjects as psychology, spiritualism, occultism, personal magnetism, and other irrational phenomena, all of which are referred to in his paintings. Moreover, these men were but two of many such whom he met at this time.

Munch seems never to have developed a fully cohesive philosophical system, but after the turn of the century his thinking turned increasingly to a consideration of the great cosmic powers, and to using them as basic themes in the monumental series of pictures done for the University of Oslo. It seems likely that he was attracted to Rudolf Steiner's philosophy, as well as other thinkers and writers who inspired the vitalism that flourished in painting and literature immediately preceding World War I.

Not infrequently Munch expresses himself in a way that recalls Nietzsche. We know that he read Nietzsche's works after 1900, although his familiarity with Nietzsche's ideas may have predated this by a decade. Kristian Schreiner, leader of Oslo University's Anatomical Institute and from the mid-1920s on a close friend of Munch's, recalls that Munch returned constantly in his monologues to his ideas about the way in which the universe is built up. "Here you could only listen to him in silent wonder" says the matter-of-fact man of science as he quotes Munch: " 'The world is one huge, living atom, It has thought-power and will-power, the clouds are its breath, the storms its mighty breathing, the glowing lava is its seething blood. Why shouldn't the sun have a will too, as it hurls its flow of light out into space? There is life and will and movement in everything, in stones and crystals as well as in the planets. The orbiting of the planets is evidence of will. And just as people's words can be sent in the form of waves through the ether, so can their thoughts travel in wave-like motion.' When, in some of his graphic work, he depicts the woman's wave-like hair functioning as the connection between her and the man, this was actually an anticipation of the discovery by a succeeding age of the existence of wave-motions in the ether.''

Where Munch speculates on such matters in his notes, he writes almost like a prose-poet. Here are some typical examples:

Are there spirits?
We see what we see because our eyes are constructed to see thus —
What are we? Energy bound in movement — a light burning — with a wick — then the inner flame — then the outer flame — and beyond that yet another invisible ring of flame — If our eyes were made differently — then, as with X-ray eyes, we'd see only our wicks — our bone structure — And if our eyes were made in still another way, we'd be able to see our outer rings of flames — see people in different forms — Why shouldn't there be other beings, less physically substantial than us — which move in and through and around us — The souls of the dead — The souls of our loved ones — and evil spirits

(*Manuscript* T 2704, uncertain date)

You inconceivable something that resides deep inside the protoplasma — in which you are like some infinitely huge head painted across the firmament — god — the inconceivable — beyond thought — the great secret — righteousness — if I have sinned — I shall be tormented forever — I did not ask for this world — no more than I asked for my skin to be white — just as the color of my hair is a matter of heredity — I have inherited my instincts and I heard a voice inside me — Man, no one is evil — Enjoy the sun — like the plants, that turn their leaves towards its light — love one another — be tolerant of one another — and when your time comes to die — when you reach the longed-for goal — then relinquish yourself gladly to the air and the earth, then rejoice

(*Manuscript* T 2782, uncertain date)

nothing is tiny, nothing is huge —
there are worlds within us — the small is part of the great as the great is part of the small —
A drop of blood is a whole world, with a sun at its center and planets — and stars — the sea is a drop of blood, a tiny part of a body — God is within us and we are within God —
— primitive and original light is everywhere, shining out wherever life is found — and
everything is movement and light —
Crystals are born and grow
like a child in the mother's womb — and the flame of life burns even in the hardest stone —
Death is the beginning of a new life
Crystallization —
Death is the beginning of life
We do not die — it is the world that
dies from us —

(*Manuscript* T 2787, probably 1895)

A short account such as this can only touch on the fascinating question of Munch's religious faith and his philosophical insights. Yet the question obviously holds great importance for us in our efforts to understand his art. Much has been written in an attempt to explain the symbolic work of the 1890s, less on the fruits of his maturity and old age. Here again we must be careful about how far we allow ourselves to go in interpretation; but the question of Munch's beliefs may be particularly relevant to his landscape paintings. Professor Schreiner's notes and quotations from Munch's own writings make it clear that Munch saw in the visible world of nature the expression of a great life-force at work, something which he wished to celebrate — a great underlying unity, a connection between all things which rendered the distinction between life and death meaningless. Insights such as these may help us to a new understanding, for instance, of the paintings of bathing scenes from the war years, in which the pale red naked bodies seem almost to be melting away into what in English is very appropriately termed "the living rock": human bodies unite with living nature beneath the life-giving rays of the sun in a world in which the distinction between the organic and the nonorganic disappears (figs. 82, 141). Thus these apparently simple bathing scenes might be seen as the poetic expression of the great order in the cosmos. Perhaps similar observations might be made about the first landscapes done at Ljan around the turn of the century (fig. 83), or about the great paintings of starry skies from the 1920s (fig. 151), or to those springtime pictures with the red barn done at Ekely in the late 1920s (figs. 156, 163), in which nature is shown once again awakening to new life and another summer.

1863. Edvard Munch born in Løten, Norway on December 12, son of military doctor Christian Munch and his wife Laura Cathrine.

1868. The artist's mother dies of tuberculosis and her sister Karen Bjølstad takes over the household.

1877. His sister Sophie dies of tuberculosis at the age of 15.

1879. Enters the Technical College with the intention of becoming an engineer.

1880. Decides to start his career as a painter.

1881. Enters the Royal Drawing School.

1882-83. Paints under the direction of Christian Krohg. Attends Frits Thaulow's "open-air academy" at Modum.

1885. First stay, three weeks, in Paris. Paints portrait of Jensen-Hjell. Begins *The Sick Child, The Day After, Puberty.* Comes into contact with the bohemian circle, led by Hans Jæger, of naturalist painters and intellectuals in Kristiania (Oslo).

1889-90. First solo exhibition in Kristiania. Paints *Inger on the Beach.* Travels to Paris on a state scholarship. Lives in Neuilly and St. Cloud while attending Léon Bonnat's art school. Sees work of the Neo-Impressionists, van Gogh, and Gauguin.

1891. Paints *Melancholy (Jappe on the Beach).*

1892. Invited to exhibit at the Verein der Berliner Künstler. After violent debate the exhibition is closed, and the resulting scandal makes Munch famous in Germany.

1893. In Berlin frequents the circle of Richard Dehmel, the poet Stanislaw Przybyszewski, Julius Meyer-Graefe, August Strindberg, and the contributors to the journal *Pan*.

1894. Produces first lithographs and etchings.

1896. Prints colored lithographs and first woodcuts at Auguste Clot's establishment in Paris. Designs lithograph for the production of *Peer Gynt* at the Théâtre de l'Oeuvre.

1897. Buys a small house in Åsgårdstrand on the Oslo fjord.

1898-1901. Travels in Germany, Italy, and France. Spends summers in Åsgårdstrand. Twice undergoes rest-visits in a sanatorium.

1902. Exhibits the *The Frieze* of *Life* in Berlin.

1906-07. Drafts décor designs for Max Reinhardt's productions of Ibsen's *Ghosts* and *Hedda Gabler.* Decorates the foyer of Reinhardt's Kammerspiele, Deutsches Theater in Berlin.

1907. Spends summer in Warnemünde on the Baltic. Paints *The Green Room, The Death of Marat,* and *Bathing Men.*

1908. Paints *Mason and Mechanic,* first of a series about modern industrial life. In the autumn suffers a nervous collapse and enters Dr. Daniel Jacobson's clinic in Copenhagen.

1909. Returns to Norway to live at Kragerø. Paints life-size portraits and landscapes. Begins designing murals for competition for the decoration of Oslo University Festival Hall.

1910. Buys the property Ramme by Hvitsten on the Oslo fjord.

1916. Buys the estate of Ekely in Skøyen outside Oslo. Oslo University unveils the murals which include *The Sun.*

1922. Paints murals for the canteen of the Freia Chocolate factory.

1930. A blood vessel bursts in Munch's right eye.

1937. Eighty-two of Munch's works are branded "degenerate" by the Germans. Munch gives financial support to the young painter Ernst Wilhelm Nay.

1940. Refuses to have any contact with the German invaders or the Quisling government.

1944. Dies on January 23 at Ekely. Bequeaths to the municipality of Oslo all of the works in his possession, including 1,000 paintings, 15,400 etchings, lithographs, and woodcuts, 4,500 watercolors and drawings, and six sculptures.

BIBLIOGRAPHY

This short list comprises titles which have been quoted or which have otherwise been of importance in composing the text of this book. Readers who wish to embark on more extensive studies are referred to the bibliography printed in Arne Eggum: *Edvard Munch. Paintings, Sketches, and Studies*, Oslo 1984.

BOOKS AND ARTICLES

Berman, Patricia G. *Edvard Munch: Mirror Reflections*. West Palm Beach: Norton Gallery & School of Art, 1986.

Bøe, Alf. "El arte de Edvard Munch después de 1900," *Edvard Munch Pintor Noruego*, exhibition catalogue Centro Cultural Arte Contemporáneo, Mexico City, 1988. First printed in *Scandinavian Review* (1986) no. 1.

Eggum, Arne. *Edvard Munch: Paintings, Sketches, & Studies*. New York: Crown Publishers, 1984. (Norwegian, German, Italian editions.)

Eggum, Arne. *Munch og fotografi*, Oslo 1987.

Elderfied, John, and Eggum, Arne. *The Masterworks of Edvard Munch*. New York: Museum of Modern Art, 1979.

Epstein, Sarah G. *The Prints of Edvard Munch: Mirror of His Life*. Edited by Jane Van Nimmen. Oberlin: Oberlin College, Allen Memorial Art Museum, 1983.

Gierløff, Christian. "Litt fra Skrubben og Ekely," *Edvard Munch. Mennesket og Kunstneren*. Oslo, 1946.

Heller, Reinhold. *Munch: His Life & Work*. Chicago: University of Chicago Press, 1986.

Hodin, J. P. *Edvard Munch*. New York: Thames & Hudson, 1985.

Kunst og Kultur, Oslo 1911 —. (Periodical — several articles on Munch.)

Langgaard, Ingrid. *Edvard Munch: Modningsår*. Oslo, 1960.

Langgaard, Johan H. & Revold, Reidar. *Edvard Munch: Auladekorasjonene*. Oslo, 1960.

Lippincott, Louise. *Edvard Munch: Starry Night*. Malibu: J. P. Getty Museum, 1988.

Messer, Thomas. *Munch*. New York: Harry N. Abrams, 1986.

Mohr, Otto Lous. *Edvard Munchs Auladekorasjoner*. Oslo, 1960.

Munch, Edvard. *Graphic Works of Edvard Munch*. New York: Dover, 1979.

Edvard Munch — Gustav Schiefler: Briefwechsel 1902-14. Vol. I. Bearbeitet von Arne Eggum et al. Hamburg, 1987.

Prelinger, Elizabeth. *Edvard Munch: Master Printmaker*. New York/London: W. W. Norton & Co., 1983.

Schiefler, Gustav. *Verzeichnis des graphischen Werks Edvard Munchs*. Vol. I, Berlin, 1907. Vol. II, Berlin, 1928. (Reprinted Oslo, 1974.)

Schreiner, Kristian E. "Minner fra Ekely," *Edvard Munch som vi kjente ham: Vennene forteller*. Oslo, 1946.

Skredsvig, Christian. *Dager og Netter blandt Kunstnere*. Oslo, 1943.

Stang, Ragna. *Edvard Munch: The Man and His Art*. Translated by Geoffrey Culverwell. New York: Abbeville Press, 1979. (Norwegian, German editions.)

Stenersen, Rolf. *Nærbilde av et geni*. Stockholm, 1944. (Quotations from 5th ed., Oslo, 1964.)

Svenæus, Gösta. *Idé och Innehåll i Edvard Munchs Konst*. Oslo, 1953.

Thiis, Jens. *Edvard Munch og hans samtid*. Oslo, 1933.

EXHIBITION CATALOGUES

Edvard Munch: Symbols and Images. National Gallery. Washington, D.C., 1978.

Edvard Munch: Der Lebensfries. Nationalgalerie. Berlin, 1978.

Edvard Munch 1863-1944. Liljevalchs Konsthall & Kulturhuset. Stockholm, 1977.

104 gravures de Edvard Munch. Fundaçao Calouste Gulbenkian. Lisbon, 1978.

Edvard Munch: Liebe, Angst und Tod. Kunsthalle Bielefeld, 1980.

Alpha & Omega. Munch Museum. Oslo, 1981. (Norwegian, German editions.)

The Artistic Revival of the Woodcut in France 1850-1900. University of Michigan Museum of Art. 1984.

Edvard Munch (1863-1944). (Published by Ministerio de Cultura, Dirección General de Bellas Artes y Archivos.) Madrid, 1984.

Edvard Munch. Museum Folkwang Essen & Kunsthaus. Zürich, 1987-88.

Edvard Munch: Sommernacht am Oslofjord, um 1900. Städtische Kunsthalle Mannheim. 1988.

Edvard Munch Pintor Noruego. Cento Cultural Arte Contemporáneo. Mexico City, 1988.

ILLUSTRATIONS

1, 2, 3. *Old Aker Church*. 1877.
Three drawings with watercolor on paper.
Munch Museum.

4. *Old Aker Church*. 1881.
Oil on board, 6⅓ × 8⅓ in. (16 × 21 cm).
Munch Museum.

5. *Landscape. Maridalen by Oslo*. 1881.
Oil on board, 8⅔ × 10⅖ in. (22 × 27.5 cm).
Munch Museum.

1

2

3

4

5

6

6. *Self-portrait*. 1881-82.
   Oil on board, 10×7⅕ in. (25.5×18.5 cm).
   Munch Museum.

7. *Aunt Karen in the Rocking Chair*. 1883.
   Oil on canvas, 18½×16 in. (47×41 cm).
   Munch Museum.

8. *Girl Kindling a Stove*. 1883.
   Oil on canvas, 38×26 in. (96.5×66 cm).
   Private collection.

9. *At the Coffee Table*. 1883.
   Oil on canvas, 18×30½ in. (45.5×77.5 cm).
   Munch Museum.

7

8

9

10. *Morning*. 1884.
    Oil on canvas, 38×40¾ in. (96.5×103.5 cm).
    Rasmus Meyer Collections, Bergen.

11. *The Sick Child*. 1885-86.
    Oil on canvas, 47×46⅔ in. (119.5×118.5 cm).
    National Gallery, Oslo.

10

8

9

10. *Morning*. 1884.
Oil on canvas, 38×40¾ in. (96.5×103.5 cm).
Rasmus Meyer Collections, Bergen.

11. *The Sick Child*. 1885-86.
Oil on canvas, 47×46⅔ in. (119.5×118.5 cm).
National Gallery, Oslo.

10

12

11

12. *Karl Jensen-Hjell*. 1885.
 Oil on canvas, 74⅖ × 39⅓ in. (190 × 100 cm).
 Private collection.

13. *Evening*. 1888.
 Oil on canvas, 29½ × 39½ in. (75 × 100.5 cm).
 Private collection.

14. *Nude, done at the studio of Léon Bonnat*. 1889.
 Charcoal.
 Munch Museum.

15. *Self-portrait*. 1886.
 Oil on canvas, 13 × 9⅔ in. (33 × 24.5 cm).
 National Gallery, Oslo.

13

14

15

16

17

16. *Hans Jæger*. 1889.
    Oil on canvas, 44×33 in. (109.5×84 cm).
    National Gallery, Oslo.

17. *Inger on the Beach*. 1889.
    Oil on canvas, 49⅖×63¾ in. (126.5×162 cm).
    Rasmus Meyer Collections, Bergen.

18. *Spring*. 1889.
    Oil on canvas, 66½×103¾ in. (169×263.5 cm).
    National Gallery, Oslo.

18

19. *Night in St. Cloud*. 1890.
    Oil on canvas, 26⅓ × 21⅓ in. (64.5 × 54 cm).
    National Gallery, Oslo.

20. *View over the River at St. Cloud*. 1890.
    Oil on canvas, 18⅓ × 15 in. (46.5 × 38 cm).
    Munch Museum.

21. *Tavern in St. Cloud*. 1890.
    Pastel on paper, 18⅖ × 25 in. (48 × 64 cm).
    Norske Selskab, Oslo.

19

20

21

22. *Spring Day on Karl Johan Street*. 1890.
Oil on canvas, 31⅓ × 39⅓ in. (80 × 100 cm).
Bergen Billedgalleri.

22

23. *Arrival of the Mail Boat.* 1890.
Oil on canvas, 38½ × 56 in. (98 × 130 cm).
Private collection.

23

24. *Rue Lafayette*. 1891.
    Oil on canvas, 36⅕ × 28¾ in. (92 × 73 cm).
    National Gallery, Oslo.

25. *Rue de Rivoli*. 1891.
    Oil on canvas, 32½ × 26 in. (82.5 × 66.5 cm).
    Fogg Art Museum, Cambridge, Massachussetts.

24

25

26. *Promenade des Anglais, Nice*. 1891.
    Oil and pastel on canvas, 21⅔ × 29 in. (55 × 74 cm).
    Private collection.

27. *By the Fireplace*. 1890-94.
    Pencil and India ink, 13⅘ × 10⅓ in. (35.1 × 26.2 cm).
    Munch Museum.

26

27

28. *Melancholy (Jappe on the Beach)*. 1892-93.
Oil on canvas, 28⅓×38½ in. (72×98 cm).
National Gallery, Oslo.

29. *Despair*. 1891.
Charcoal and gouache on paper, 14½×16⅓ in. (37×42.2 cm).
Munch Museum.

28

29

30

30. *The Painter Jacob Bratland*. 1891-92.
Oil on canvas, 39⅓ × 26 in. (100 × 66 cm).
Munch Museum.

31. *August Strindberg*. 1892.
Oil on canvas, 47⅕ × 35⅖ in. (120 × 90 cm).
Museum of Modern Art, Stockholm.

31

32. *The Mystery of a Summer Night.* 1892.
Oil on canvas, 34 × 49 in. (86.5 × 124.5 cm).
Private collection.

33. *Moonlight on the Shore.* 1892.
Oil on canvas, 24⅔ × 37¾ in. (62.5 × 96 cm).
Rasmus Meyer Collections, Bergen.

34. *Evening on Karl Johan Street*. 1892.
Oil on canvas, 33⅕ × 47⅔ in. (84.5 × 121 cm).
Rasmus Meyer Collections, Bergen.

35. *By the Roulette*. 1892.
Oil on canvas, 29⅓ × 45⅖ in. (74.5 × 115.5 cm).
Munch Museum.

34

35

36. *Dagny Juel Przybyszewska*. 1893.
Oil on canvas, 58½ × 39⅙ in. (148.5 × 99.5 cm).
Munch Museum.

37. *By the Deathbed (Fever)*. 1893.
Pastel on board, 23⅔ × 31½ in. (60 × 80 cm).
Munch Museum.

36

37

38. *The Storm*. 1893.
   Oil on canvas, 36 × 51½ in. (91.5 × 131 cm).
   Museum of Modern Art, New York.

39. *The Scream*. 1893.
   Tempera and pastel on board, 35⅘ × 29 in. (91 × 73.5 cm).
   National Gallery, Oslo.

38

36. *Dagny Juel Przybyszewska*. 1893.
   Oil on canvas, 58½ × 39⅙ in. (148.5 × 99.5 cm).
   Munch Museum.

37. *By the Deathbed (Fever)*. 1893.
   Pastel on board, 23⅔ × 31½ in. (60 × 80 cm).
   Munch Museum.

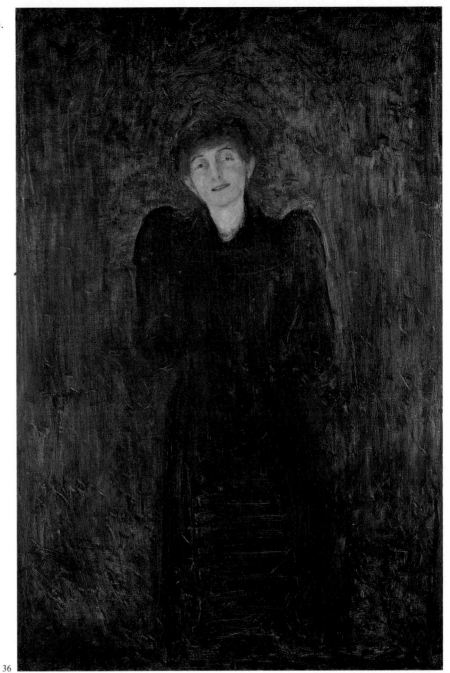

36

37

38. *The Storm*. 1893.
 Oil on canvas, 36 × 51½ in. (91.5 × 131 cm).
 Museum of Modern Art, New York.

39. *The Scream*. 1893.
 Tempera and pastel on board, 35⅘ × 29 in. (91 × 73.5 cm).
 National Gallery, Oslo.

38

40. *Rose and Amélie.* 1893.
Oil on canvas, 30¾ × 43 in. (78 × 109 cm).
Munch Museum.

41. *Young Man and a Prostitute.* 1893.
Charcoal and gouache, 19⅔ × 18⅘ in. (50 × 47.8 cm).
Munch Museum.

42. *Hands.* c. 1893.
Oil on board, 35⅘ × 30⅓ in. (91 × 77 cm).
Munch Museum.

43. *The Voice.* c. 1893.
Oil on canvas, 35⅗ × 46⅔ in. (90 × 118.5 cm).
Munch Museum.

40

41

42

43

44. *Vampire*. 1893-94.
   Oil on canvas, 35⅘ × 43 in. (91 × 109 cm).
   Munch Museum.

45. *Separation*. 1894.
   Oil on canvas, 45¼ × 59 in. (115 × 150 cm).
   Munch Museum.

44

45

46. *Anxiety*. 1894.
Oil on canvas, 37 × 28¾ in. (94 × 73 cm).
Munch Museum.

47. *Woman in Three Stages*. 1894.
   Oil on canvas, 64½×98⅖ in. (164×250 cm).
   Rasmus Meyer Collections, Bergen.

47

48. *Ashes*. 1894.
Oil and tempera on canvas, 47⅖ × 55½ in. (120.5 × 141 cm).
National Gallery, Oslo.

49. *The Sick Child*. 1894.
Drypoint, 14⅓ × 11 in. (36.5 × 27.9 cm).
Munch Museum.

50. *Death and the Maiden*. 1894.
Drypoint, 11⅓ × 8 in. (28.8 × 20.2 cm).
Munch Museum.

48

49

50

51. *Puberty*. 1894.
    Oil on canvas, 59⅔ × 43⅓ in. (151.5 × 110 cm).
    National Gallery, Oslo.

52. *Eye in Eye*. 1894.
    Oil on canvas, 53½ × 43⅓ in. (136 × 110 cm).
    Munch Museum.

53. *The Day After*. 1894-95.
Oil on canvas, 45¼ × 59⅔ in. (115 × 152 cm).
National Gallery, Oslo.

54. *Madonna*. 1894-95.
Oil on canvas, 35⅘ × 27¾ in. (91 × 70.5 cm).
National Gallery, Oslo.

55. *The Kiss*. 1895.
Etching, aquatint and drypoint, 52⅓ × 10⅓ in. (32.9 × 26.2 cm).
Munch Museum.

56. *Death in the Sickroom*. Probably 1894-95.
Oil on canvas, 59 × 66 in. (150 × 167.5 cm).
National Gallery, Oslo.

57. *Death in the Sickroom*. 1896.
Lithograph, 15⅓ × 21⅔ in. (39 × 55 cm).
Munch Museum.

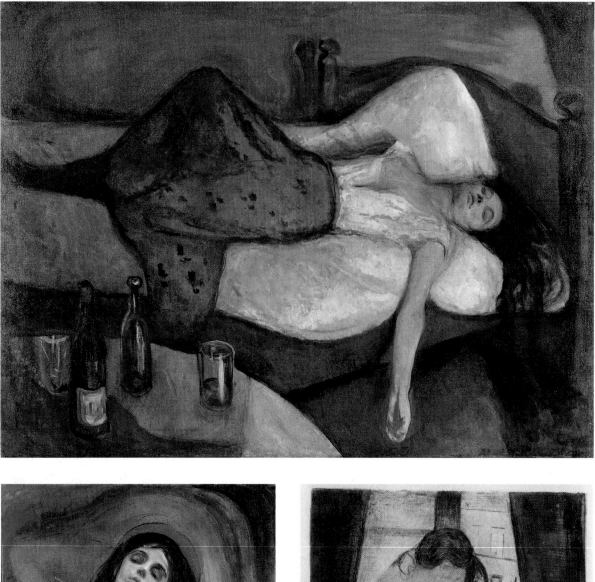

53

54

55

56

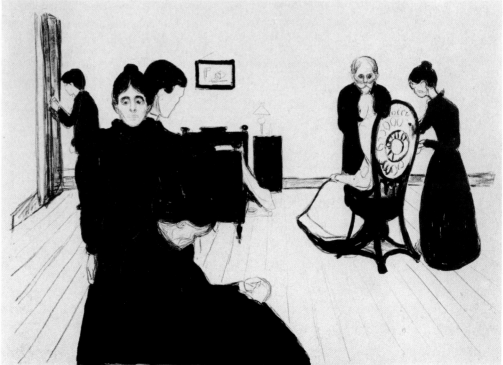

57

58

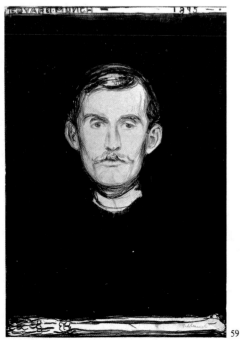

59

60

58. *Self-portrait with Cigarette.* 1895.
   Oil on canvas, 43½ × 33⅔ in. (110.5 × 85.5 cm).
   National Gallery, Oslo.

59. *Self-portrait with Skeleton Arm.* 1895.
   Lithograph, 18 × 12½ in. (45.5 × 31.7 cm).
   Munch Museum.

60. *The Scream.* 1895.
   Lithograph, 14 × 10 in. (35.5 × 25.4 cm).
   Munch Museum.

61. *Jealousy.* 1895.
   Oil on canvas, 26⅓ × 39⅓ in. (67 × 100 cm).
   Rasmus Meyer Collections, Bergen.

62. *Jealousy I.* 1896.
   Lithograph, 12⅘ × 18¹⁄₁₀ in. (32.6 × 46 cm).
   Munch Museum.

61

62

63. *Stanislaw Przybyszewski.* 1895.
Tempera on canvas, 29½ × 23⅔ in. (75 × 60 cm).
Munch Museum.

64. *August Strindberg.* 1896.
Lithograph, 23⅔ × 18⅒ in. (60 × 46 cm).
Munch Museum.

65. *Vampire.* 1895-1902.
Combined woodcut and lithograph, 15⅙ × 21¾ in. (38.5 × 55.3 cm).
Munch Museum.

66. *Anxiety.* 1896.
Woodcut, 18 × 14¾ in. (45.7 × 37.5 cm).
Munch Museum.

63

64

65

66

67. *The Sick Child*. 1896.
Lithograph, 16⅘ × 22⅔ in. (42.8 × 57.5 cm).
Munch Museum.

68. *Beneath the Yoke*. 1896.
Engraving, 9¼ × 8⅖ in. (23.5 × 21.4 cm).
Munch Museum.

69. *Attraction*. 1896.
Lithograph, 18⅔ × 14¼ in. (47.4 × 36.3 cm).
Munch Museum.

67

68

69

70. *Girl on the Beach*. 1896.
Aquatint with scraper and drypoint on zinc,
11¹/₁₀ × 8½ in. (28.2 × 21.7 cm).
Munch Museum.

71. *The Flower of Pain*. 1897.
India ink, wash, watercolor and crayon,
19²/₃ × 16⁹/₁₀ in. (50 × 43 cm).
Designed for the front page of the magazine *Quickborn*.
Munch Museum.

72. *The Kiss*. 1897-98.
Woodcut, 23¼ × 18 in. (59.1 × 45.7 cm).
Munch Museum.

73. *The Kiss*. 1898.
Woodcut, 17½ × 17½ in. (44.7 × 44.7 cm).
Munch Museum.

70

72

71

73

67. *The Sick Child*. 1896.
Lithograph, 16⅘ × 22⅔ in. (42.8 × 57.5 cm).
Munch Museum.

68. *Beneath the Yoke*. 1896.
Engraving, 9¼ × 8⅖ in. (23.5 × 21.4 cm).
Munch Museum.

69. *Attraction*. 1896.
Lithograph, 18⅔ × 14¼ in. (47.4 × 36.3 cm).
Munch Museum.

67

68

69

70. *Girl on the Beach*. 1896.
    Aquatint with scraper and drypoint on zinc,
    11¹⁄₁₀ × 8½ in. (28.2 × 21.7 cm).
    Munch Museum.

71. *The Flower of Pain*. 1897.
    India ink, wash, watercolor and crayon,
    19⅔ × 16⁹⁄₁₀ in. (50 × 43 cm).
    Designed for the front page of the magazine *Quickborn*.
    Munch Museum.

72. *The Kiss*. 1897-98.
    Woodcut, 23¼ × 18 in. (59.1 × 45.7 cm).
    Munch Museum.

73. *The Kiss*. 1898.
    Woodcut, 17½ × 17½ in. (44.7 × 44.7 cm).
    Munch Museum.

70

72

71

73

74. *The Kiss*. 1897.
Oil on canvas, $39 \times 31^{9}/_{10}$ in. (99×81 cm).
Munch Museum.

75. *The Dead Mother and the Child.* 1897-99.
    Oil on canvas, 41⅙×70⅔ in. (104.5×179.5 cm).
    Munch Museum.

76. *The Lonely Ones.* 1899.
    Woodcut, 15½×20⅘ in. (39.5×53 cm).
    Munch Museum.

75

76

77. *Fertility I*. 1898.
    Oil on canvas, 47¼ × 55¹⁄₁₀ in. (120 × 140 cm).
    Private collection.

78. *Red Virginia Creeper*. 1898-1900.
    Oil on canvas, 47 × 47⅔ in. (119.5 × 121 cm).
    Munch Museum.

79. *Metabolism*. 1899.
    Oil on canvas, 67⁹⁄₁₀ × 55⁹⁄₁₀ in. (172.5 × 142 cm).
    Munch Museum.

80

81

80. *The Dance of Life*. 1899-1900.
Oil on canvas,
49⅖ × 75 in. (125.5 × 190.5 cm).
National Gallery, Oslo.

81. *Golgotha*. 1900.
Oil on canvas, 31½ × 47¼ in. (80 × 120 cm).
Munch Museum.

82. *Man Bathing*. 1899.
Woodcut, 17⅓ × 17⅓ in. (44 × 44 cm).
Munch Museum.

83. *White Night*. 1901.
Oil on canvas, 45½ × 43½ in. (115.5 × 110.5 cm).
National Gallery, Oslo.

84. *Train Smoke*. 1900.
Oil on canvas, 33¼ × 42⁹⁄₁₀ in. (84.5 × 109 cm).
Munch Museum.

82

83

84

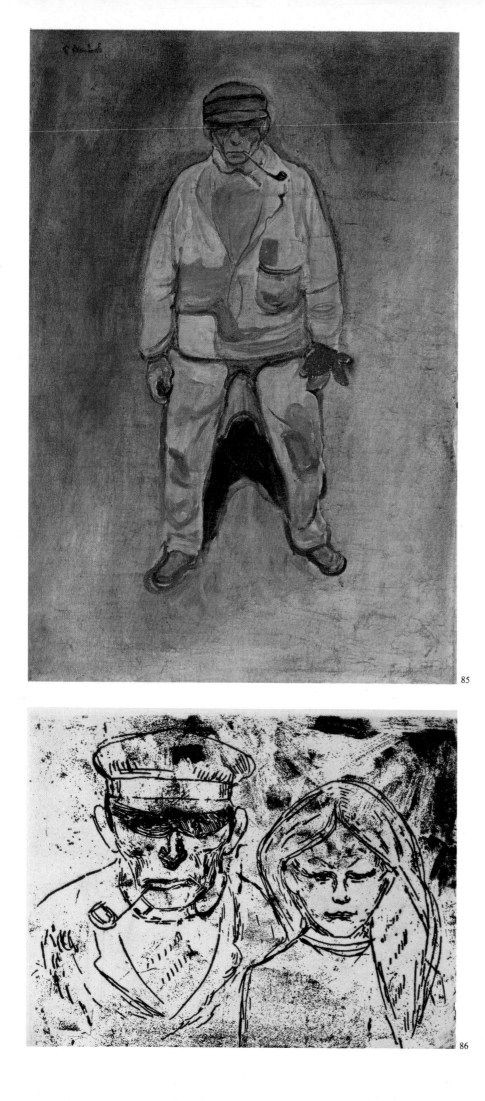

85

86

85. *The Fisherman.* c. 1902.
Oil on canvas, 35 × 24 in. (89 × 61 cm).
Munch Museum.

86. *The Fisherman and His Daughter.* 1902.
Engraving, 18¾ × 24⅒ in. (47.5 × 61.3 cm).
Munch Museum.

87. *The Girls on the Bridge.* 1901.
Oil on canvas, 53½ × 49⅖ in. (136 × 125.5 cm).
National Gallery, Oslo.

87

88. *Albert Kollmann*. 1902.
Oil on canvas, 32 × 25¾ in. (81.5 × 65.5 cm).
Kunsthaus Zürich.

89. *Forest*. 1903.
Oil on canvas, 32½ × 32 in. (82.5 × 81.5 cm).
Munch Museum.

90. *Rain*. 1902.
Oil on canvas, 34 × 45½ in. (86.5 × 115.5 cm).
National Gallery, Oslo.

91. *Fertility II*. 1902.
Oil on canvas, 50⅓ × 59⅘ in. (128 × 152 cm).
Munch Museum.

92. *The Brooch. Eva Mudocci*. 1903.
Lithograph, 23⅔ × 18¹⁄₁₀ in. (60 × 46 cm).
Munch Museum.

93. *Dr. Linde's House*. 1902.
Etching, 17½ × 21⅘ in. (44.6 × 55.5 cm).
Munch Museum.

88

89

90

91

92

93

94. *The Ladies on the Bridge*. 1902.
Oil on canvas, 72⅖ × 80¾ in. (184 × 205 cm).
Bergen Billedgalleri.

95. *The Ladies on the Bridge*. 1903.
Oil on canvas, 79⁹⁄₁₀ × 90½ in. (203 × 230 cm).
Thielska Galleriet, Stockholm.

94

95

96

97

96. *Dr. Max Linde's Four Sons*. 1903.
   Oil on canvas, 56⅔ × 78½ in. (144 × 199.5 cm).
   Museum Behnhaus, Lübeck.

97. *Trees on the Shore. Panel from the Linde Frieze*. 1904.
   Oil on canvas, 36⅔ × 65¾ in. (93 × 167 cm).
   Munch Museum.

98. *Harry Graf Kessler*. 1904.
   Oil on canvas, 33⅘ × 29½ in. (86 × 75 cm).
   Private collection.

99. *Ludvig Karsten*. 1905.
   Oil on canvas, 76⅓ × 35⅘ in. (194 × 91 cm).
   Thielska Galleriet, Stockholm.

98

99

100

96. *Dr. Max Linde's Four Sons.* 1903.
Oil on canvas, 56⅔ × 78½ in. (144 × 199.5 cm).
Museum Behnhaus, Lübeck.

97. *Trees on the Shore. Panel from the Linde Frieze.* 1904.
Oil on canvas, 36⅔ × 65¾ in. (93 × 167 cm).
Munch Museum.

98. *Harry Graf Kessler.* 1904.
Oil on canvas, 33⅘ × 29½ in. (86 × 75 cm).
Private collection.

99. *Ludvig Karsten.* 1905.
Oil on canvas, 76⅓ × 35⅘ in. (194 × 91 cm).
Thielska Galleriet, Stockholm.

98

99

100. *Self-portrait with Brushes*. 1904.
Oil on canvas, 77½ × 36 in. (197 × 91.5 cm).
Munch Museum.

101. *Four Girls in Åsgårdstrand*. 1904-05.
Oil on canvas, 34¼ × 43⅓ in. (87 × 110 cm).
Munch Museum.

102. *Caricature of Munch's earlier friends — his mistress Tulla
Larsen with writers Gunnar Heiberg (as toad) and Sigurd
Bødtker (as dog)*. 1905.
Engraving, 2½ × 3¾ in. (6.5 × 9.5 cm).
Munch Museum.

103. *Man and Woman*. 1905.
Woodcut, 15⅘ × 21¼ in. (40.3 × 54 cm).
Munch Museum.

101

102

103

104. *From Thüringerwald*. c. 1905.
    Oil on canvas, 31½ × 39⅓ in. (80 × 100 cm).
    Munch Museum.

105. *The Murderess*. 1906.
    Oil on canvas, 27⅓ × 39⅓ in. (69.5 × 100 cm).
    Munch Museum.

104

105

106. *Self-portrait in Weimar.* 1906.
Oil on canvas, 43½ × 47⅖ in. (110.5 × 120.5 cm).
Munch Museum.

107

108

109

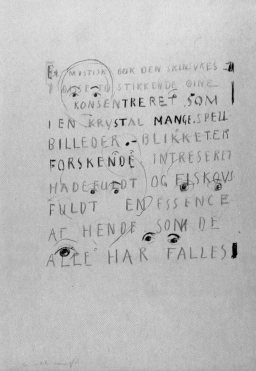

107. *The Murderess*. 1906.
    Oil on canvas, 43⅓ × 47¼ in. (110 × 120 cm).
    Munch Museum.

108. *Old Man in Warnemünde*. 1907.
    Oil on canvas, 43⅓ × 33⅖ in. (110 × 85 cm).
    Munch Museum.

109. *Weeping Girl. Study for the Reinhardt Frieze*. 1906-07.
    Tempera on canvas, 36¼ × 56¼ in. (92 × 143 cm).
    Munch Museum.

110. *Page from The Tree of Knowledge of Good and Evil*.
    Colored crayon on paper, 25¾ × 18¾ in. (65.3 × 47.5 cm).
    Munch Museum.

110

111. *Walther Rathenau*. 1907.
Oil on canvas, 86⅔ × 43⅓ in. (220 × 110 cm).
Rasmus Meyer Collections, Bergen.

112. *Jealousy*. From the series *The Green Room*. 1907.
Oil on canvas, 29⁹⁄₁₀ × 38½ in. (76 × 98 cm).
Munch Museum.

113. *Brothel Scene. Zum süssen Mädel*. From the series *The Green Room*. 1907.
Oil on canvas, 33⅖ × 51½ in. (85 × 131 cm).
Munch Museum.

112

113

114. *The Death of Marat*. 1907.
Oil on canvas, 59 × 78¾ in. (150 × 200 cm).
Munch Museum.

115. *Bathing Men*. 1907.
Oil on canvas, 81¹/₁₀ × 109½ in. (206 × 277 cm).
Athenaeum Art Museum, Helsinki.

114

115

116. *Worker and Child*. 1908.
Oil on canvas, 29⁹⁄₁₀ × 35⅖ in. (76 × 90 cm).
Munch Museum.

117. *The Nurse*. 1908-09.
Engraving, 8 × 5⅔ in. (20.4 × 14.4 cm).
Munch Museum.

118. *Self-portrait at Professor Jacobson's Hospital*. 1909.
Oil on canvas, 39⅓ × 43⅓ in. (100 × 110 cm).
Rasmus Meyer Collections, Bergen.

119. *Omega and the Pig*. From the series *Alpha and Omega*. 1908-09.
Lithograph, 12½ × 14⅖ in. (31.7 × 36.6 cm).
Munch Museum.

116

117

118

119

120. *Christen Sandberg.* 1909.
Oil on canvas, 84⅔ × 57⅘ in. (215 × 147 cm).
Munch Museum.

121. *Professor Daniel Jacobson.* 1909.
Oil on canvas, 80⅓ × 43⁹⁄₁₀ in. (204 × 111.5 cm).
Munch Museum.

121

122. *Thorvald Stang*. 1909.
Oil on canvas, 79½ × 38 in. (202 × 96.5 cm).
Munch Museum.

123. *Jens Thiis*. 1909.
Oil on canvas, 79⁹⁄₁₀ × 40⅙ in. (203 × 102 cm).
Munch Museum.

124. *Christian Gierloff*. 1910.
Oil on canvas, 80¾ × 38½ in. (205 × 98 cm).
Gothenburg Art Museum.

122

123

124

125

126

125. *The Murderer*. 1910.
Oil on canvas, 37⅕ × 60⅔ in. (94.5 × 154 cm).
Munch Museum.

126. *The Yellow Log*. 1911-12.
Oil on canvas, 51½ × 63 in. (131 × 160 cm).
Munch Museum.

127. *Galloping Horse*. 1910-12.
Oil on canvas, 58¼ × 47 in. (148 × 119.5 cm).
Munch Museum.

128. *The Sun*. From the Oslo University Aula decorations. 1911-16.
Oil on canvas, 177⅙ × 307 in. (450 × 780 cm).

129. *Awakening Men*. From the Oslo University Aula decorations. 1911-16.
Oil on canvas, 179 × 120 in. (455 × 305 cm).

128

129

130. *Alma Mater*. From the Oslo University Aula decorations. 1911-16.
Oil on canvas, 179 1/10 × 456 5/8 in. (455 × 1160 cm).

131. *History*. From the Oslo University Aula decorations. 1911-16.
Oil on canvas, 177 1/6 × 457 4/5 in. (450 × 1163 cm).

130

131

132. *Winter in Kragerø*. 1912.
Oil on canvas, 51¾×51½ in. (131.5×131 cm).
Munch Museum.

132

133. *Man and Woman II*. 1912-15.
   Oil on canvas, 35 × 45½ in. (89 × 115.5 cm).
   Munch Museum.

134. *Nude*. c. 1913.
   Oil on canvas, 31½ × 39⅓ in. (80 × 100 cm).
   Munch Museum.

133

134

135. *Workers in the Snow.* c. 1913.
Oil on canvas, 64⅙ × 78¾ in. (163 × 200 cm).
Munch Museum.

136. *Workers on Their Way Home.* 1913-15.
Oil on canvas, 79¹⁄₁₀ × 89⅓ in. (201 × 227 cm).
Munch Museum.

135

137. *The Logger.* 1913.
Oil on canvas, 51⅛×41½ in. (130×105.5 cm).
Munch Museum.

138. *The Bite.* 1913.
Etching, 7¾×11 in. (19.8×27.9 cm).
Munch Museum.

139. *The Dance of Anitra, sketch for Henrik Ibsen's play* Peer Gynt. 1913.
Color crayon, 14×10¼ in. (35.5×26 cm).
Munch Museum.

137

138

139

140. *By the Deathbed (Fever)*. c. 1915.
Oil on canvas, 73⅔ × 92⅒ in. (187 × 234 cm).
Munch Museum.

140

141. *High Summer II*. 1915.
Oil on canvas, 37⅖ × 47 in. (95 × 119.5 cm).
Munch Museum.

142. *Ragnarok IV*. 1915.
Lithograph, 7⁹⁄₁₀ × 8⅙ in. (20.2 × 20.7 cm).
Munch Museum.

143. *Europe United*. 1916.
Lithograph, 16¹⁄₁₀ × 9⅘ in. (40.9 × 25 cm).
Munch Museum.

141

142

143

144. *Spring Plowing*. 1916.
Oil on canvas, $33 \times 42^{9}/_{10}$ in. (84×109 cm).
Munch Museum.

145. *Metabolism*. c. 1916.
Hand-colored lithograph, $27^{2}/_{3} \times 19^{2}/_{3}$ in. (70.3×50 cm).
Munch Museum.

146. *The Tree*. 1916.
Lithograph, $8^{2}/_{3} \times 14$ in. (21.9×35.5 cm).
Munch Museum.

144

145

146

147. *The Artist and His Model*. 1919-21.
Oil on canvas, 52¾ × 62½ in. (134 × 159 cm).
Munch Museum.

148. *Self-portrait after the Spanish Flu*. 1919.
Oil on canvas, 59¼ × 51½ in. (150.5 × 131 cm).
National Gallery, Oslo.

149

150

149. *Model by the Wicker Chair*. 1919-21. Oil on canvas, 48¼ × 39⅓ in. (122.5 × 100 cm). Munch Museum.

150. *The Human Mountain, Ragnarok* and *The Rainbow* in the Garden at Ekely, probably late 1920s. Munch Museum.

151. *Starry Night*. 1923-24. Oil on canvas, 54¾ × 46⅘ in. (139 × 119 cm). Munch Museum.

152. *Outing at Grefsenåsen*. 1921. Color crayon on paper, 5⁹⁄₁₀ × 10⅔ in. (15.1 × 26.9 cm). Munch Museum.

151

152

153

154

153. *Model on the Couch*. 1924-28.
   Oil on canvas, 53¾ × 45½ in. (136.5 × 115.5 cm).
   Munch Museum.

154. *Osvald and Mrs. Alving, sketch for final scene from Henrik*
   Ibsen's play Ghosts. 1920.
   Lithograph, 15⅓ × 19⅔ in. (39 × 50 cm).
   Munch Museum.

155. *The Wedding of the Bohemian, Munch seated on far left*. 1925.
   Oil on canvas, 54⅓ × 71¼ in. (138 × 181 cm).
   Munch Museum.

155

156. *Red Barn and Spruces*. c. 1927.
Oil on canvas, 39⅓ × 51⅕ in. (100 × 130 cm).
Munch Museum.

157. *Building of the Oslo City Hall*. 1929 or earlier.
Watercolor, 27½ × 39⅓ in. (70 × 100 cm).
Munch Museum.

158. *H. F. Frölich*. 1930-31.
Woodcut and board, 34¼ × 25⅔ in. (87 × 65 cm).
Munch Museum.

159. *Building the Winter Studio, Ekely*. 1929.
Oil on canvas, 58⅔ × 45¼ in. (149 × 115 cm).
Munch Museum.

156

157

158

159

160. *The Lonely Ones*. c. 1935.
Oil on canvas, 39⅓ × 51⅓ in. (100 × 130 cm).
Munch Museum.

161. *The Ladies on the Bridge*. c. 1935.
Oil on canvas, 47 × 51 in. (119.5 × 129.5 cm).
Munch Museum.

160

162. *Hans Jæger*. 1943.
    Lithograph, 15 × 12⅖ in. (38 × 31.5 cm).
    Munch Museum.

163. *Spring Landscape with Red House*. c. 1935.
    Oil on canvas, 39⅓ × 51⅕ in. (100 × 130 cm).
    Munch Museum.

164. *Self-portrait Between the Clock and the Bed*. 1940-42.
    Oil on canvas, 58⅘ × 47¼ in. (149.5 × 120 cm).
    Munch Museum.

162

163

LIST OF ILLUSTRATIONS

60. *The Scream*. 1895.
Lithograph, 14×10 in. (35.5×25.4 cm).
Munch Museum.

61. *Jealousy*. 1895.
Oil on canvas, $26\frac{1}{3} \times 39\frac{1}{3}$ in. (67×100 cm).
Rasmus Meyer Collections, Bergen.

62. *Jealousy I*. 1896.
Lithograph, $12\frac{4}{5} \times 18\frac{1}{10}$ in. (32.6×46 cm).
Munch Museum.

63. *Stanislaw Przybyszewski*. 1895.
Tempera on canvas,
$29\frac{1}{2} \times 23\frac{2}{3}$ in. (75×60 cm).
Munch Museum.

64. *August Strindberg*. 1896.
Lithograph, $23\frac{2}{3} \times 18\frac{1}{10}$ in. (60×46 cm).
Munch Museum.

65. *Vampire*. 1895-1902.
Combined woodcut and lithograph,
$15\frac{1}{6} \times 21\frac{3}{4}$ in. (38.5×55.3 cm).
Munch Museum.

66. *Anxiety*. 1896.
Woodcut, $18 \times 14\frac{3}{4}$ in. (45.7×37.5 cm).
Munch Museum.

67. *The Sick Child*. 1896.
Lithograph, $16\frac{4}{5} \times 22\frac{2}{3}$ in. (42.8×57.5 cm).
Munch Museum.

68. *Beneath the Yoke*. 1896.
Engraving, $9\frac{1}{4} \times 8\frac{2}{5}$ in. (23.5×21.4 cm).
Munch Museum.

69. *Attraction*. 1896.
Lithograph, $18\frac{2}{3} \times 14\frac{1}{4}$ in. (47.4×36.3 cm).
Munch Museum.

70. *Girl on the Beach*. 1896.
Aquatint with scraper and drypoint on zinc,
$11\frac{1}{10} \times 8\frac{1}{2}$ in. (28.2×21.7 cm).
Munch Museum.

71. *The Flower of Pain*. 1897.
India ink, wash, watercolor and crayon,
$19\frac{2}{3} \times 16\frac{9}{10}$ in. (50×43 cm).
Designed for the front page of the magazine *Quickborn*.
Munch Museum.

72. *The Kiss*. 1897-98.
Woodcut, $23\frac{1}{4} \times 18$ in. (59.1×45.7 cm).
Munch Museum.

73. *The Kiss*. 1898.
Woodcut, $17\frac{1}{2} \times 17\frac{1}{2}$ in. (44.7×44.7 cm).
Munch Museum.

74. *The Kiss*. 1897.
Oil on canvas, $39 \times 31\frac{9}{10}$ in. (99×81 cm).
Munch Museum.

75. *The Dead Mother and the Child*.
1897-99.
Oil on canvas,
$41\frac{1}{6} \times 70\frac{2}{3}$ in. (104.5×179.5 cm).
Munch Museum.

76. *The Lonely Ones*. 1899.
Woodcut, $15\frac{1}{2} \times 20\frac{4}{5}$ in. (39.5×53 cm).
Munch Museum.

77. *Fertility I*. 1898.
Oil on canvas, $47\frac{1}{4} \times 55\frac{1}{10}$ in. (120×140 cm).
Private collection.

78. *Red Virginia Creeper*. 1898-1900.
Oil on canvas, $47 \times 47\frac{2}{3}$ in. (119.5×121 cm).
Munch Museum.

79. *Metabolism*. 1899.
Oil on canvas,
$67\frac{9}{10} \times 55\frac{9}{10}$ in. (172.5×142 cm).
Munch Museum.

80. *The Dance of Life*. 1899-1900.
Oil on canvas,
$49\frac{2}{5} \times 75$ in. (125.5×190.5 cm).
National Gallery, Oslo.

81. *Golgotha*. 1900.
Oil on canvas, $31\frac{1}{2} \times 47\frac{1}{4}$ in. (80×120 cm).
Munch Museum.

82. *Man Bathing*. 1899.
Woodcut, $17\frac{1}{3} \times 17\frac{1}{3}$ in. (44×44 cm).
Munch Museum.

83. *White Night*. 1901.
$45\frac{1}{2} \times 43\frac{1}{2}$ in. (115.5×110.5 cm).
National Gallery, Oslo.

84. *Train Smoke*. 1900.
Oil on canvas, $33\frac{1}{4} \times 42\frac{9}{10}$ in. (84.5×109 cm).
Munch Museum.

85. *The Fisherman*. c. 1902.
Oil on canvas, 35×24 in. (89×61 cm).
Munch Museum.

86. *The Fisherman and His Daughter*. 1902.
Engraving, $18\frac{3}{4} \times 24\frac{1}{10}$ in. (47.5×61.3 cm).
Munch Museum.

87. *The Girls on the Bridge*. 1901.
Oil on canvas, $53\frac{1}{2} \times 49\frac{2}{5}$ in. (136×125.5 cm).
National Gallery, Oslo.

88. *Albert Kollmann*. 1902.
Oil on canvas, $32 \times 25\frac{3}{4}$ in. (81.5×65.5 cm).
Kunsthaus Zürich.

89. *Forest*. 1903.
Oil on canvas, $32\frac{1}{2} \times 32$ in. (82.5×81.5 cm).
Munch Museum.

90. *Rain*. 1902.
Oil on canvas, $34 \times 45\frac{1}{2}$ in. (86.5×115.5 cm).
National Gallery, Oslo.

91. *Fertility II*. 1902.
Oil on canvas, $50\frac{1}{3} \times 59\frac{4}{5}$ in. (128×152 cm).
Munch Museum.

92. *The Brooch. Eva Mudocci*. 1903.
Lithograph, $23\frac{2}{3} \times 18\frac{1}{10}$ in. (60×46 cm).
Munch Museum.

93. *Dr. Linde's House*. 1902.
Etching, $17\frac{1}{2} \times 21\frac{4}{5}$ in. (44.6×55.5 cm).
Munch Museum.

94. *The Ladies on the Bridge*. 1902.
Oil on canvas, $72\frac{2}{5} \times 80\frac{3}{4}$ in. (184×205 cm).
Bergen Billedgalleri.

95. *The Ladies on the Bridge*. 1903.
Oil on canvas, $79\frac{9}{10} \times 90\frac{1}{2}$ in. (203×230 cm).
Thielska Galleriet, Stockholm.

96. *Dr. Max Linde's Four Sons*. 1903.
Oil on canvas, $56\frac{2}{3} \times 78\frac{1}{2}$ in. (144×199.5 cm).
Museum Behnhaus, Lübeck.

97. *Trees on the Shore. Panel from the Linde Frieze*. 1904.
Oil on canvas, $36\frac{2}{3} \times 65\frac{3}{4}$ in. (93×167 cm).
Munch Museum.

98. *Harry Graf Kessler*. 1904.
Oil on canvas, $33\frac{4}{5} \times 29\frac{1}{2}$ in. (86×75 cm).
Private collection.

99. *Ludvig Karsten*. 1905.
Oil on canvas, $76\frac{1}{3} \times 35\frac{4}{5}$ in. (194×91 cm).
Thielska Galleriet, Stockholm.

100. *Self-portrait with Brushes*. 1904.
Oil on canvas, $77\frac{1}{2} \times 36$ in. (197×91.5 cm).
Munch Museum.

101. *Four Girls in Åsgårdstrand*. 1904-05.
Oil on canvas, $34\frac{1}{4} \times 43\frac{1}{3}$ in. (87×110 cm).
Munch Museum.

102. *Caricature of Munch's earlier friends — his mistress Tulla Larsen with writers Gunnar Heiberg (as toad) and Sigurd Bødtker (as dog)*. 1905.
Engraving, $2\frac{1}{2} \times 3\frac{3}{4}$ in. (6.5×9.5 cm).
Munch Museum.

103. *Man and Woman*. 1905.
Woodcut, $15\frac{4}{5} \times 21\frac{1}{4}$ in. (40.3×54 cm).
Munch Museum.

104. *From Thüringerwald*. c. 1905.
Oil on canvas, $31\frac{1}{2} \times 39\frac{1}{3}$ in. (80×100 cm).
Munch Museum.

105. *The Murderess*. 1906.
Oil on canvas, $27\frac{1}{3} \times 39\frac{1}{3}$ in. (69.5×100 cm).
Munch Museum.

106. *Self-portrait in Weimar*. 1906.
Oil on canvas,
$43\frac{1}{2} \times 47\frac{2}{5}$ in. (110.5×120.5 cm).
Munch Museum.

107. *The Murderess*. 1906.
Oil on canvas, $43\frac{1}{3} \times 47\frac{1}{4}$ in. (110×120 cm).
Munch Museum.

108. *Old Man in Warnemünde*. 1907.
Oil on canvas, $43\frac{1}{3} \times 33\frac{2}{5}$ in. (110×85 cm).
Munch Museum.

109. *Weeping Girl. Study for the Reinhardt Frieze*. 1906-07.
Tempera on canvas,
$36\frac{1}{4} \times 56\frac{1}{4}$ in. (92×143 cm).
Munch Museum.

110. *Page from The Tree of Knowledge* of *Good and Evil*.
Colored crayon on paper,
$25\frac{3}{4} \times 18\frac{3}{4}$ in. (65.3×47.5 cm).
Munch Museum.

111. *Walther Rathenau*. 1907.
Oil on canvas, $86\frac{2}{3} \times 43\frac{1}{3}$ in. (220×110 cm).
Rasmus Meyer Collections, Bergen.

112. *Jealousy*. From the series *The Green Room*. 1907.
Oil on canvas, $29\frac{9}{10} \times 38\frac{1}{2}$ in. (76×98 cm).
Munch Museum.

113. *Brothel Scene. Zum süssen Mädel*.
From the series *The Green Room*. 1907.
Oil on canvas, $33\frac{2}{5} \times 51\frac{1}{2}$ in. (85×131 cm).
Munch Museum.

114. *The Death of Marat*. 1907.
Oil on canvas, 59 × 78¾ in. (150 × 200 cm).
Munch Museum.

115. *Bathing Men*. 1907.
Oil on canvas, 81¹/₁₀ × 109½ in. (206 × 277 cm).
Athenaeum Art Museum, Helsinki.

116. *Worker and Child*. 1908.
Oil on canvas, 29⁹/₁₀ × 35⅖ in. (76 × 90 cm).
Munch Museum.

117. *The Nurse*. 1908-09.
Engraving, 8 × 5⅔ in. (20.4 × 14.4 cm).
Munch Museum.

118. *Self-portrait at Professor Jacobson's Hospital*. 1909.
Oil on canvas, 39⅓ × 43⅓ in. (100 × 110 cm).
Rasmus Meyer Collections, Bergen.

119. *Omega and the Pig*. From the series *Alpha and Omega*. 1908-09.
Lithograph, 12½ × 14⅖ in. (31.7 × 36.6 cm).
Munch Museum.

120. *Christen Sandberg*. 1909.
Oil on canvas, 84⅔ × 57⅘ in. (215 × 147 cm).
Munch Museum.

121. *Professor Daniel Jacobson*. 1909.
Oil on canvas, 80⅓ × 43⁹/₁₀ in. (204 × 111.5 cm).
Munch Museum.

122. *Thorvald Stang*. 1909.
Oil on canvas, 79½ × 38 in. (202 × 96.5 cm).
Munch Museum.

123. *Jens Thiis*. 1909.
Oil on canvas, 79⁹/₁₀ × 40⅙ in. (203 × 102 cm).
Munch Museum.

124. *Christian Gierløff*. 1910.
Oil on canvas, 80¾ × 38½ in. (205 × 98 cm).
Gothenburg Art Museum.

125. *The Murderer*. 1910.
Oil on canvas, 37⅕ × 60⅔ in. (94.5 × 154 cm).
Munch Museum.

126. *The Yellow Log*. 1911-12.
Oil on canvas, 51½ × 63 in. (131 × 160 cm).
Munch Museum.

127. *Galloping Horse*. 1910-12.
Oil on canvas, 58¼ × 47 in. (148 × 119.5 cm).
Munch Museum.

128. *The Sun*. From the Oslo University Aula decorations. 1911-16.
Oil on canvas, 177⅙ × 307 in. (450 × 780 cm).

129. *Awakening Men*. From the Oslo University Aula decorations. 1911-16.
Oil on canvas, 179 × 120 in. (455 × 305 cm).

130. *Alma Mater*. From the Oslo University Aula decorations. 1911-16.
Oil on canvas, 179¹/₁₀ × 456⅝ in. (455 × 1160 cm).

131. *History*. From the Oslo University Aula decorations. 1911-16.
Oil on canvas, 177⅙ × 457⅘ in. (450 × 1163 cm).

132. *Winter in Kragerø*. 1912.
Oil on canvas, 51¾ × 51½ in. (131.5 × 131 cm).
Munch Museum.

133. *Man and Woman II*. 1912-15.
Oil on canvas, 35 × 45½ in. (89 × 115.5 cm).
Munch Museum.

134. *Nude*. c. 1913.
Oil on canvas, 31½ × 39⅓ in. (80 × 100 cm).
Munch Museum.

135. *Workers in the Snow*. c. 1913.
Oil on canvas, 64⅙ × 78¾ in. (163 × 200 cm).
Munch Museum.

136. *Workers on Their Way Home*. 1913-15.
Oil on canvas, 79¹/₁₀ × 89⅓ in. (201 × 227 cm).
Munch Museum.

137. *The Logger*. 1913.
Oil on canvas, 51⅙ × 41½ in. (130 × 105.5 cm).
Munch Museum.

138. *The Bite*. 1913.
Etching, 7¾ × 11 in. (19.8 × 27.9 cm).
Munch Museum.

139. *The Dance of Anitra, sketch for Henrik Ibsen's play* Peer Gynt. 1913.
Color crayon, 14 × 10¼ in. (35.5 × 26 cm).
Munch Museum.

140. *By the Deathbed (Fever)*. c. 1915.
Oil on canvas, 73⅔ × 92¹/₁₀ in. (187 × 234 cm).
Munch Museum.

141. *High Summer II*. 1915.
Oil on canvas, 37⅖ × 47 in. (95 × 119.5 cm).
Munch Museum.

142. *Ragnarok IV*. 1915.
Lithograph, 7⁹/₁₀ × 8⅙ in. (20.2 × 20.7 cm).
Munch Museum.

143. *Europe United*. 1916.
Lithograph, 16¹/₁₀ × 9⅘ in. (40.9 × 25 cm).
Munch Museum.

144. *Spring Plowing*. 1916.
Oil on canvas, 33 × 42⁹/₁₀ in. (84 × 109 cm).
Munch Museum.

145. *Metabolism*. c. 1916.
Hand-colored lithograph,
27⅔ × 19⅔ in. (70.3 × 50 cm).
Munch Museum.

146. *The Tree*. 1916.
Lithograph, 8⅔ × 14 in. (21.9 × 35.5 cm).
Munch Museum.

147. *The Artist and His Model*. 1919-21.
Oil on canvas, 52¾ × 62½ in. (134 × 159 cm).
Munch Museum.

148. *Self-portrait after the Spanish Flu*. 1919.
Oil on canvas, 59¼ × 51½ in. (150.5 × 131 cm).
National Gallery, Oslo.

149. *Model by the Wicker Chair*. 1919-21.
Oil on canvas, 48¼ × 39⅓ in. (122.5 × 100 cm).
Munch Museum.

150. *The Human Mountain, Ragnarok* and *The Rainbow* in the Garden at Ekely, probably late 1920s.
Munch Museum.

151. *Starry Night*. 1923-24.
Oil on canvas, 54¾ × 46⅘ in. (139 × 119 cm).
Munch Museum.

152. *Outing at Grefsenåsen*.
1921.
Color crayon on paper,
5⁹/₁₀ × 10⅔ in. (15.1 × 26.9 cm).
Munch Museum.

153. *Model on the Couch*. 1924-28.
Oil on canvas,
53¾ × 45½ in. (136.5 × 115.5 cm).
Munch Museum.

154. *Osvald and Mrs. Alving, sketch for final scene from Henrik Ibsen's play Ghosts*. 1920.
Lithograph, 15⅓ × 19⅔ in. (39 × 50 cm).
Munch Museum.

155. *The Wedding of the Bohemian, Munch seated on far left*. 1925.
Oil on canvas, 54⅓ × 71¼ in. (138 × 181 cm).
Munch Museum.

156. *Red Barn and Spruces*. c. 1927.
Oil on canvas, 39⅓ × 51⅕ in. (100 × 130 cm).
Munch Museum.

157. *Building of the Oslo City Hall*.
1929 or earlier.
Watercolor, 27½ × 39⅓ in. (70 × 100 cm).
Munch Museum.

158. *H. F. Frölich*. 1930-31.
Woodcut and board,
34¼ × 25⅔ in. (87 × 65 cm).
Munch Museum.

159. *Building the Winter Studio, Ekely*. 1929.
Oil on canvas, 58⅔ × 45¼ in. (149 × 115 cm).
Munch Museum.

160. *The Lonely Ones*. c. 1935.
Oil on canvas, 39⅓ × 51⅕ in. (100 × 130 cm).
Munch Museum.

161. *The Ladies on the Bridge*. c. 1935.
Oil on canvas, 47 × 51 in. (119.5 × 129.5 cm).
Munch Museum.

162. *Hans Jæger*. 1943.
Lithograph, 15 × 12⅖ in. (38 × 31.5 cm).
Munch Museum.

163. *Spring Landscape with Red House*.
c. 1935.
Oil on canvas, 39⅓ × 51⅕ in. (100 × 130 cm).
Munch Museum.

164. *Self-portrait Between the Clock and the Bed*. 1940-42.
Oil on canvas, 58⅘ × 47¼ in. (149.5 × 120 cm).
Munch Museum.